In No Time

Excel
2000

IN NO TIME

Rainer Walter Schwabe

AN IMPRINT OF PEARSON EDUCATION

PEARSON EDUCATION LIMITED

Head Office:
Edinburgh Gate
Harlow CM20 2JE
Tel: +44 (0) 1279 623623
Fax: +44 (0) 1279 431059

London Office:
128 Long Acre
London WC2E 9AN
Tel: +44 (0) 171 447 2000
Fax: +44 (0) 171 240 5771

First published in Great Britain in 2000
© Pearson Education Limited 2000

First published in 1999 as *Excel 2000: leicht, klar, sofort*
by Markt & Technik Buch- und Software-Verlag GmbH
Martin-Kollar-Straße 10–12
D-81829 Munich
GERMANY

Library of Congress Cataloging in Publication Data
Available from the publisher.

British Library Cataloguing in Publication Data
A CIP catalogue record for this book can be obtained from the British Library.

ISBN 0-130-16222-1

10   9   8   7   6   5   4   3   2   1

Translated and typeset by Cybertechnics, Sheffield.
Printed and bound in Great Britain by Henry Ling Ltd, at The Dorset Press, Dorchester, Dorset.

The publishers' policy is to use paper manufactured from sustainable forests.

Contents

4 The first spreadsheet _____ 68

Private Budget

Income		
Net Income		£5,000
Rent		£1,000
Interest		£0.40
Sum of income		=SUM(C5:C8)+C5:C8

5 Storing and printing _____ 90

Private Budget

Income

	5000
	1000
	50
	6050

6 Accessing, saving, and deleting workbooks ___ 112

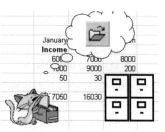

January

Income

600	7000	8000
800	9000	200
50	30	
7050	16030	

7 Copying and filling cells 130

8 Copying calculations the easy way 150

	Turnover Adam	Turnover Miller	Turnover Smith	Turnover Zimmer
April	10000	40000	15000	20000
May	20000	10000	5000	5000
June	30000	20000	2500	2000

9 Currencies and the euro converter 160

10 Everything as a percentage   186

Amounts	Per cent
£1,000.00	12%
£ 500.00	6%
£ 300.00	3%
£2,300.00	27%
£4,500.00	52%

11 Your first charts   202

12 The first functions   228

Maximum

Average

Minimum

13 If, ... then Excel will ...! 258

14 Indices for overviews 304

15 Help, help, help! 322

Appendices   332

Index   377

Dear Reader

Never forget that mighty oaks from tiny acorns grow. Let's start at the beginning by asking the question 'What is Excel?'

With the help of numerous examples this book will acquaint you step by step with Excel.

My aim is to help you to get over the initial inhibitions which are always experienced by beginners embarking on something new.

The chapters are designed to be useful in practice, too.

I would advise you to have a go at the tasks. They not only reinforce your knowledge, but also outline new paths.

Finally, I would like to thank all participants of my introductory courses to Excel. They have not only shown me which problems are experienced by beginners, but also inspired me to write this book. My particular thanks to those participants who 'didn't know the first thing' about Windows when they started, who thought a mouse was vermin, and who, as the course progressed, really got into Excel.

I am sure you will become just as enthusiastic about Excel as my 'guinea pigs'. That is why after reading the book you, too, will be able to say:

'Excel – I learnt it IN NO TIME!'

Incidentally, if you like it and you want to learn Word, have a look at Word 2000 In No Time.

Yours

Rainer Walter Schwabe

The following three pages show you how your computer keyboard is structured. Groups of keys are dealt with one by one to make it easier to understand.

Most of the computer keys are operated exactly as keys on a typewriter. However, there are a few additional keys, which are designed for the peculiarities of computer work.

See for yourself ...

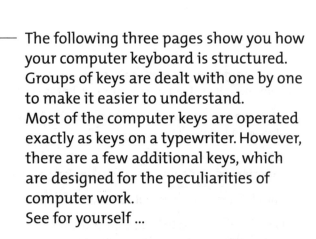

Typewriter keys

Use these keys exactly as you do on a typewriter.
The Enter key is also used to send commands to your computer.

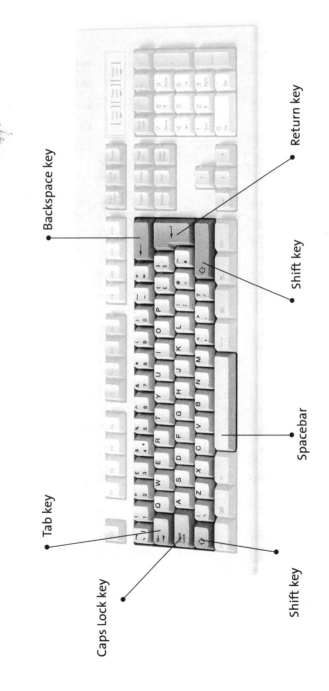

Tab key

Caps Lock key

Shift key

Backspace key

Return key

Shift key

Spacebar

Special keys, function keys, status lights, numeric key pad

Special keys and function keys are used for special tasks in computer operation. Ctrl-, Alt- and AltGr keys are usually used in combination with other keys. The Esc key can cancel commands, Insert and Delete can be used, amongst other things, to insert and delete text.

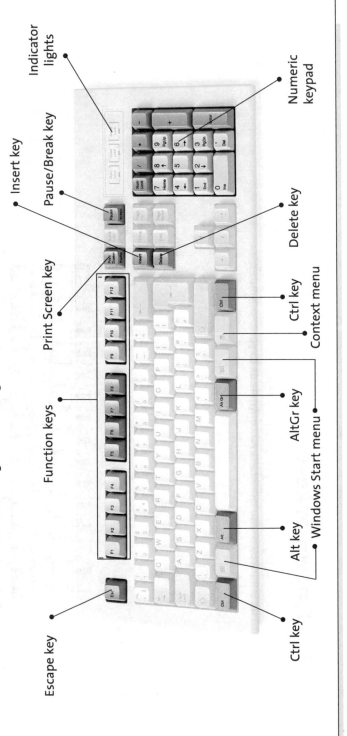

Escape key

Function keys

Print Screen key

Pause/Break key

Insert key

Indicator lights

Numeric keypad

Delete key

Ctrl key

Context menu

AltGr key

Windows Start menu

Alt key

Ctrl key

Navigation keys

These keys are used to move around the screen.

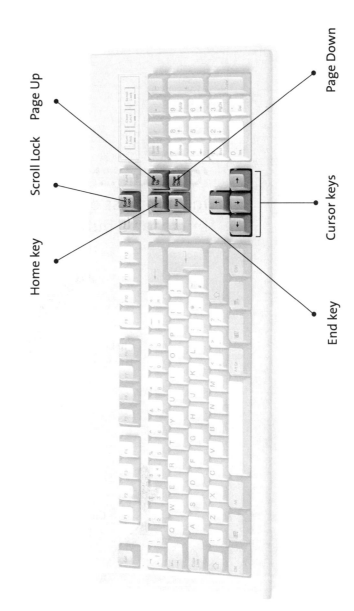

Page Up

Scroll Lock

Home key

Page Down

Cursor keys

End key

'Click on ...'

means: press once
briefly on a button.

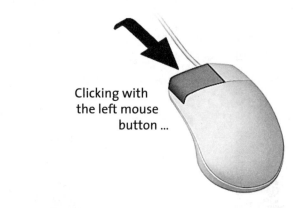

Clicking with
the left mouse
button ...

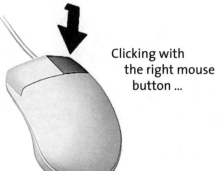

Clicking with
the right mouse
button ...

'Double-click on ...'

means: press the left button twice briefly in quick succession

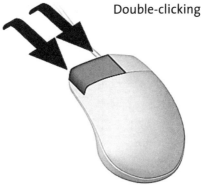

Double-clicking

'Drag ...'

means: click on an object with the left mouse button, keep the button pressed, move the mouse and thus drag the item to another position.

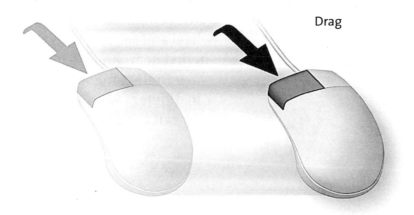

Drag

What's in this chapter?

In life there is a first time for everything, or so they say: the first baby steps, the first day at school, the first best friend, the first kiss, the first disappointment, ... and the first time you work with Excel! Just as every experienced driver has had to take driving lessons first, a beginner takes his first steps in Excel. Sit down behind the steering wheel and set off slowly in first gear: you will learn how to start the software in different ways and how to exit the program!

You are going to learn about:

Starting Excel

Before you can carry out your first calculations in Excel, you need to launch the application. This is one of the easiest ways of doing it: Excel 2000 is a **program**. As with most programs, you first click on the START button in Windows . This button is located in the bottom left corner of your screen.

Excel has automatically been created as a separate menu item in the roll-up menu list, after successful installation. This is where you start the software on your screen.

The following procedures are the same for starting any other Office 2000 applications, such as Word, PowerPoint, Outlook or Access.

1 Click on START. The **Start menu** opens.

	Open Office Document
	Programs
	Favorites
	Documents
	Settings
	Find

2 Select.

3 Windows opens an additional window, a so-called **SUB-MENU**. Click on MICROSOFT EXCEL: the program will now be launched.

After start-up, the **user interface** of Excel 2000 is displayed.

A **USER interface** is how a program looks on your screen.

Switching off the Assistant!

When you first start-up the software, a bubbly **Assistant** immediately appears on the screen. In this case it is a paper clip. It will help you with using the software. This little helper can be very useful, though occasionally it makes a nuisance of itself.

You are going to learn more about this funny 'freak' later (Chapter 15 'Help, help, help!'). For the moment you should switch it off.

1 Move the mouse pointer onto the Assistant.

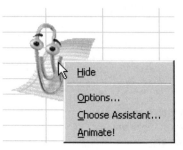

Hide

Options...
Choose Assistant...
Animate!

2 Press the right mouse button.

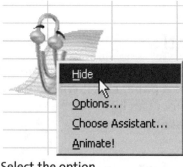

Hide

Options...
Choose Assistant...
Animate!

3 Select the option HIDE ASSISTANT from the Context menu.

For now, your 'little helper' has disappeared from the screen.

Exiting Excel

With the Menu bar, commands such as EXIT or PRINT are called up, by first left-clicking on the File menu and then selecting (clicking on) the appropriate option in the open menu.

Now that you have started Excel, close it down again. In this way you will familiarise yourself with the first steps. To exit the program, use the **Menu bar**.

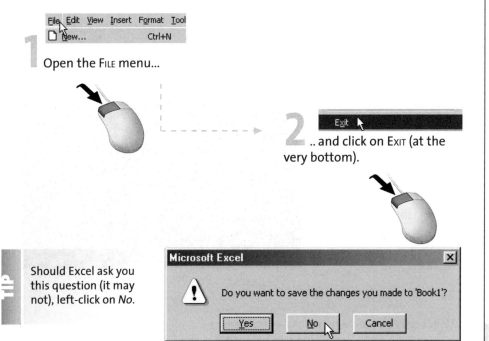

Open the FILE menu...

2 .. and click on EXIT (at the very bottom).

Should Excel ask you this question (it may not), left-click on *No*.

As you have not entered anything important, you do not need to **SAVE** (storing of data) anything yet. (More about saving can be found in Chapter 5 'Storing and printing'!) If you clicked on the *Cancel* button, you return to Excel as if nothing had happened.

Alternatives for starting and exiting Excel

'There's more than one way to skin a cat!' This also applies to starting Excel 2000. A very easy way would be to create a separate **icon** for Excel on the Windows user interface, the so-called **desktop**.

Creating an icon for Excel!

Surely you have already noticed the icons. When you **double-click** on one, the associated program is launched on your screen. Such a connection or start-up option is referred to as a **link**.

For Excel – that is, for starting the program – you can create such a link yourself. You will need need to use the (Ctrl) key, which is found on your keyboard, together with the left mouse button.

1

Place the mouse pointer on START, and press the **right** mouse button first.

2 Choose OPEN.

Programs

3 Click on *Programs*.

Microsoft Excel   Microsoft Exchange

Microsoft PowerPoint   Microsoft Publisher

4 Click on 'Microsoft Excel', and keep the left mouse button pressed down.

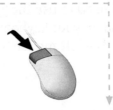

5 Press the Ctrl key.

6 With the left mouse button, drag the Excel icon onto the Windows desktop.

As soon as you release the Ctrl key first and then the left mouse button, the icon appears on the Windows desktop.

When you **double-click** on the new link, Excel is launched from here, too.

Holding down the left mouse button, you can move the icon to any point on the desktop.

Alternatives for exiting Excel

Two more options: you can exit Excel directly by either **double-clicking** on the **Excel icon** (top left) or **left-clicking once** on the **cross (X)** in the top right.

TIP

You can exit Excel with the **keyboard**, too, by first pressing the [Alt] key and then the [F4] key.

WHAT'S THIS?

The combined pressing of two or more keys is called a **keyboard shortcut**. It executes one particular function.

You are probably thinking that so far you have not done anything with Excel! You have learnt – just like in your first driving lesson – how to start and switch off the engine.

Well, let's start the engine – oh, sorry – the program and open the book at Chapter 2 'The first steps: cells and numbers'. You are setting off in first gear.

17

2

the first steps: cells and numbers

What's in this chapter?

Start Excel, and you will see a totally new world on your screen, a world which is as alien to you as earth must have been to ET, or Mars to NASA, a world you will want to explore.

How is Excel structured and what is the meaning of all those 'buttons' and 'grey surfaces'? You enter the first numbers. What can you do   when you have entered a wrong value (for example, instead of '4711' '4712')? This chapter will show you!

	A	B	C
1	123	456	789
2			
3			
4			
5			

You already know about:

You are going to learn about:

At first sight!

Microsoft Excel is a program for working with **spreadsheet**. On the screen, a table is displayed which consists of **columns** and **rows**. This is where your calculations are carried out.

Calculate = 'compute, assess'. Derived from the Latin word *calculare* (the literal translation is: to handle counting stones).

Where are you?

'In front of my computer!' might be your first answer to that question. But let's be serious about this point: in Excel, it is very important to know where the mouse pointer is.

The screen is divided into two main areas. These are the command area and the work area.

At the very top you will find the **command** area. Here, as the name implies, commands are called up and executed with the **mouse** or with the **keyboard**.

You can also see the work area. In Excel, this area is referred to as the **worksheet**.

On a **worksheet**, you can carry out your calculations (or enter numbers and text).

Pay attention to appearances!

The mouse pointer always indicates its current position. It literally communicates (in sign language) with you, and informs you what you are able to do at that moment – commands or entries.

Its appearance changes according to its position on the screen. If your mouse pointer is in the **command area**, it appears as an arrow. Now you can execute actions like SAVING, PRINTING, and so on.

 In contrast, when you position the mouse pointer on the **worksheet**, it turns into a white cross. Now you can enter data, such as numbers and/or text.

Move the mouse pointer across the command area, ...

A comprehensive overview of the various shapes of the mouse pointer and their meaning can be found in the Appendix 'The mouse pointer and its appearance'.

... and then across the work area, that is the table.

Activating and deactivating individual toolbars

You will get to know more about the individual toolbars in the course of the book, when you will have to work with the individual commands!

In the command area you can find various toolbars:

Menu toolbar

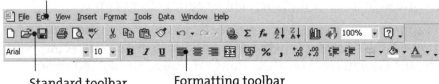

Standard toolbar   Formatting toolbar

If the individual toolbars are not displayed as above, you must instruct Excel to tile them horizontally. For this, you will use the TOOLS/CUSTOMIZE menu option.

1 In the *Tools* menu select ...

2 ... CUSTOMIZE.

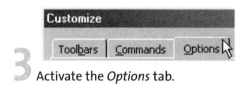

3 Activate the *Options* tab.

Here you can determine the appearance of your screen. Tile the toolbars either vertically or horizontally.

Vertically or horizontally?

Effect on the screen

Effect on the screen

Standard toolbar

Formatting toolbar

If there is a tick in front of the entry, click on it. In this way the toolbars will be tiled horizontally.

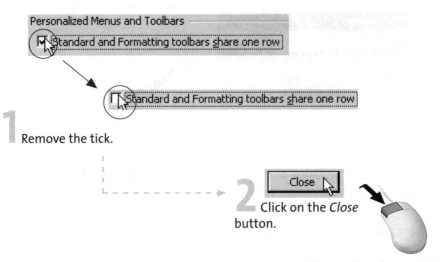

1 Remove the tick.

2 Click on the *Close* button.

With beginners, especially, the question arises: 'Do I really have to know the names of all these Toolbars?'. The answer is: yes!

Just consider this real-life example . If you are taking driving lessons, you must know what the words 'clutch', 'brakes' and 'accelerator' mean when your driving instructor uses these terms. Nobody has ever said: 'Now slowly release the first pedal from the left!'

Some toolbars might not be present on your screen (especially when several people share one computer).

In Excel 2000 you can **activate** or **deactivate** individual toolbars. For this, you will use the VIEW/TOOLBARS menu option.

There should be a **tick** against **Standard** and **Formatting**. This means that both are activated. When you click on an item, you switch off the corresponding toolbar on your screen.

The **Standard** and **Formatting toolbar** should be activated on your screen. They enable you to call up commands more quickly.

1 Open the VIEW menu, and select TOOLBARS.

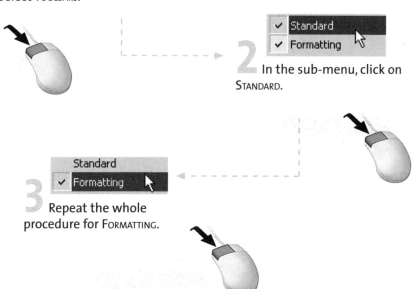

2 In the sub-menu, click on STANDARD.

3 Repeat the whole procedure for FORMATTING.

Both toolbars have disappeared from your screen. You can activate them again with the same method.

Another option: place the mouse pointer anywhere on a toolbar and press the right mouse button.

WHAT'S THIS?

The name **Context menu** refers to the fact that the composition of the individual menu items depends on what you are doing when you press the right mouse button. Each command can also be executed via the Menu bar.

A menu opens – to be precise – a **Context menu** in which you can also activate/deactivate the toolbars.

25

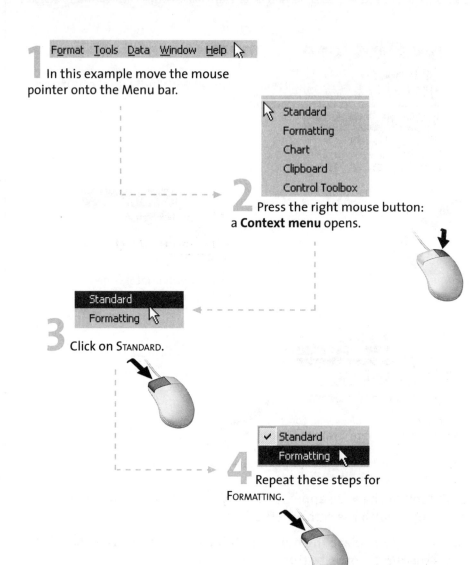

1 Format Tools Data Window Help

In this example move the mouse pointer onto the Menu bar.

Standard
Formatting
Chart
Clipboard
Control Toolbox

2 Press the right mouse button: a **Context menu** opens.

Standard
Formatting

3 Click on STANDARD.

✓ Standard
Formatting

4 Repeat these steps for FORMATTING.

The toolbars – Standard and Formatting, in this case – are again displayed on your screen.

ScreenTips for beginners

Excel assists you in getting better acquainted with individual commands of the Standard and Formatting Toolbars.

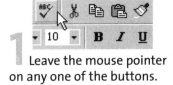

1 Leave the mouse pointer on any one of the buttons.

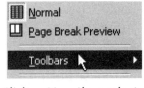

2 After approximately one second **ScreenTips** is displayed.

You will see a short **description** as to what would happen if you clicked on that button.

CAUTION

If ScreenTips is not displayed, you, as a beginner, should really activate it with the following procedure. This makes you first steps in Excel easier, because it helps you to memorise the Toolbars function much faster!

1 Click on VIEW, then select
TOOLBARS.

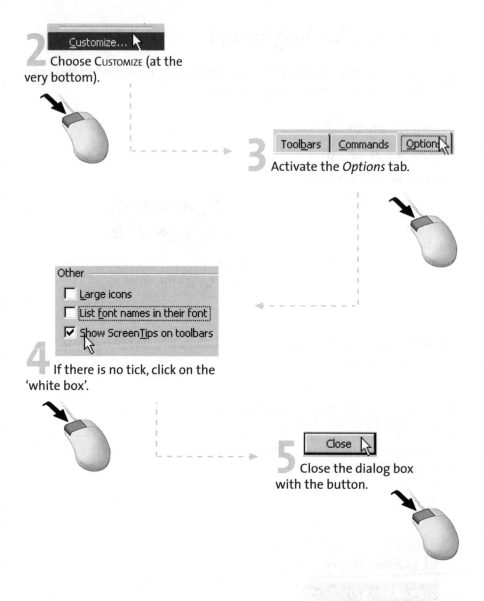

2 Choose CUSTOMIZE (at the very bottom).

3 Activate the *Options* tab.

4 If there is no tick, click on the 'white box'.

5 Close the dialog box with the button.

Place the mouse pointer – without pressing the mouse button – on a button. Result: ScreenTips is displayed.

Clicking on a check box modifies the settings of Excel 2000.

A tick appears in the box, which is called **check box**, after you have clicked on it: the function has been activated.

☑ Show ScreenTips on toolbars

What is a dialog box?

You have worked with a **dialog box**. This is where you instruct Excel about what you would like to change (in this case: activating ScreenTips).

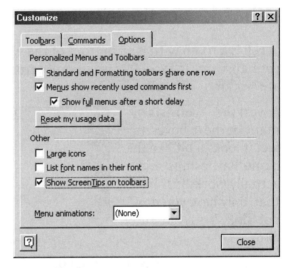

Dialog boxes are used to enter data and to select commands. This means that a dialog is actually taking place between you as the user and Excel.

What are tabs?

To structure **dialog boxes** reasonably clearly, many are designed as a kind of card-index file containing various tabs.

During the last procedure you have, for the first time within this book, worked with tabs. These work just as in a **card index**.

Cards can be selected by clicking on the tab name of the appropriate card. We can refer to the cards as 'tabs', as they are really one and the same thing, for practical purposes. Do not confuse the use of the word 'tab' in this case with the Tab key on the keyboard.

Instead of turning over the pages, you simply click on the **name** (the tab) of the appropriate card with the mouse. The card is then automatically moved to the front.

| Tool**b**ars | **C**ommands | Option**s** |

What is a cell?

'A cell is a room with bars in front of the window', might be one of your answers. In Excel this is not quite true: when you enter data you are working with **cells**.

A worksheet consists of many of these boxes. In fact it looks a bit like the game 'Battleships' and actually works just like that, only here you do not 'sink ships', but enter data.

	A	B	C	D	E
1					
2					
3					
4					
5					
6					
7					

In Excel the intersection points where a column and a row meet are called **cells**.

The individual boxes are intersection points between columns and rows .

The cell **names** are derived from the **intersection points** between individual columns and rows.

A cell name lists the **column** first and then the **row**.

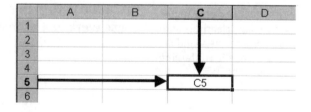

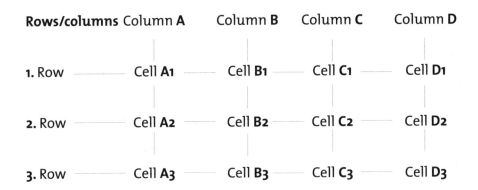

Rows/columns	Column **A**	Column **B**	Column **C**	Column **D**
1. Row	Cell **A1**	Cell **B1**	Cell **C1**	Cell **D1**
2. Row	Cell **A2**	Cell **B2**	Cell **C2**	Cell **D2**
3. Row	Cell **A3**	Cell **B3**	Cell **C3**	Cell **D3**

From cell to cell

You get from one cell to the next by simply clicking on the new one with the mouse.

The highlighted black **box** indicates the **cell** you are currently in. This is where you enter your data.

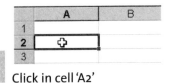

Click in cell 'A2'

Select a new cell.

You can use the following options to move within a worksheet on the screen.

The left mouse button

The Cursor keys

The Tab(ulator) key

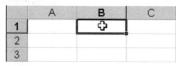

1 Click on cell 'B1'.

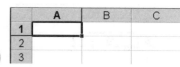

2 Press the ← key. In this way you move one cell to the left.

3 With the ↓ key you move to cell 'A2'.

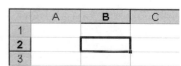

4 When you press the ⇆ key, you move to the right to cell 'B2'.

Entering numbers

The purpose of a spreadsheet is the **calculation** of numbers. For our purpose, only Arabic numbers count as numbers. The values always appear in individual cells. For example, click on a cell with the mouse. You can only enter data (numbers, text or later formulas) in a cell, on which you have clicked so that it is selected.

TIP

Type the appropriate numbers on the keyboard. As soon as you have entered the first digit, the cursor starts flashing in the cell.

WHAT'S THIS?

The cursor is an on-screen **position indicator** in the form of a flashing vertical line. It marks the place where the next entry will appear.

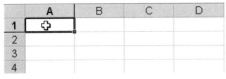

Click on the top left cell (= A1).

With the keyboard, enter the number '12'.

Excel thus knows that you have completed your entries and that the number is supposed to appear in the cell.

A 'type of confirmation' is provided when the **number** is moved to the **right** by the program.

→ 123

	A	**B**	C	D
1	12			
2				
3				
4				

1 Press the Tab key once. You have moved to the right into cell 'B1'.

	A	**B**	C	D
1	12	56		
2				
3				
4				

2 Enter '56'.

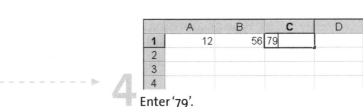

3 Press the → cursor key. You move to cell 'C1'.

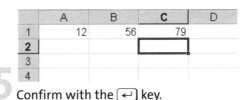

4 Enter '79'.

When you complete your entry with the ↵ key, you automatically move down one cell (in this example to 'C2')!

	A	B	C	D
1	12	56	79	
2				
3				
4				

5 Confirm with the ↵ key.

The Formula bar

Help with **entering data** is provided by the **Formula bar**. As the name implies, it displays what you are currently editing. It is thus also referred to as 'entry row'.

You get precise information!

On the Formula bar you will see the **name** of the cell (A1, A2, B1, B2 ...), which is active at the moment. You can also see its **contents**. When you click on the number '12' which you have already entered, you can see it in the Formula bar, too.

The Formula bar provides information about:

Concept	Example
Cell name	A1
Cell contents	12

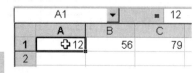

Click on cell 'A1'.

Select cell 'C1'.

However, when you select an empty cell, only its name is displayed on the Formula bar (here 'B2').

While you are entering data ...

... you will notice a cross and a tick on the Formula bar, as well as the name and the contents of the cell.

	A	B	C	D
1	12	56	79	
2				
3				

Click on cell 'A2'.

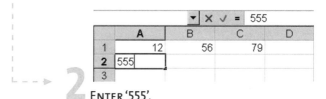

ENTER '555'.

Clicking on the **cross** on the Formula bar (or pressing the [Esc] key on your keyboard) **cancels** your current entry.

Delete the number

A2			=	
	A	B	C	D
1	12	56	79	
2				
3				

... and the **unfinished** entry again.

When you activate the tick on the Formula bar, you confirm the **entry**.

37

	A	B	C	D
1	12	56	79	
2	666			
3				
4				

1 Enter the number '666'.

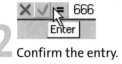

The Formula bar is one of the best ways to make entries.

2 Confirm the entry.

Correcting numbers

'Nobody is perfect!' Surely you have made mistakes before. Hardly anybody can claim that he or she only ever makes correct entries.

'Making mistakes – oh, sorry – mistakes are only human!'

You do not need to enter everything again, but you can correct the mistake.

Overwriting a cell

You want to change the value completely! Click on it and enter the new data.

Example:

In cell 'A2' you can see the value '666'. You wish to replace it with '777'.

A2	▼	=	666

	A	B	C	D
1	12	56	79	
2	⊕ 666			
3				

1 Click (if necessary) on cell 'A2'.

A2	▼	× ✓	=	777

	A	B	C	D
1	12	56	79	
2	777			
3				

2 Type the number '777' on the keyboard.

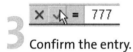

3 Confirm the entry.

Deleting cells (cell contents)

You can also delete cells – to be more precise, cell contents – completely, by pressing the Del key on the keyboard.

Example:

You wish to delete the contents of cell 'A2' completely.

A2	▼	=	777

	A	B	C	D
1	12	56	79	
2	⊕777			
3				

1 Click (if necessary) on cell 'A2'.

39

A2	▼	=	
	A	B	C	D
1	12	56	79	
2				
3				

2 Press the Del key.

Correcting cell contents

Instead of entering cell contents again, you can simply correct them. Here the Formula bar comes in very handy.

Example:

You wish to change the contents of cell 'A1' from '12' to '123'. Simply insert a '3' after the digits that you have already entered.

CELL NAME	**CURRENT CELL CONTENTS**	**CHANGE TO:**
A1	12	123

A1	▼	=	12	
	A	B	C	D
1	⊹ 12	56	79	
2				
3				
4				

1 Select cell 'A1'.

2 On the Formula bar, click after the digit '2'.

3 Type the number '3'.

4 Activate any cell to confirm the entry.

Example:

You wish to correct the contents of cell 'B1' to '456'. Thus, you have to insert a digit in front of the existing value '56'.

CELL NAME	CURRENT CELL CONTENTS	CHANGE TO:
B1	56	456

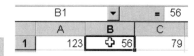

1 Click on cell 'B1'.

2

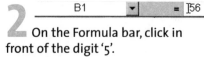

On the Formula bar, click in front of the digit '5'.

3 Insert the number '4'.

4 Confirm the entry by clicking on a cell.

Example:

You wish to change the contents of cell 'C1' from '79' to '789' and you do it by inserting a new digit between the existing ones.

CELL NAME	CURRENT CELL CONTENTS	CHANGE TO:
C1	79	789

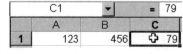

1 Click on cell 'C1'.

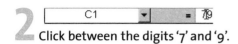

2 Click between the digits '7' and '9'.

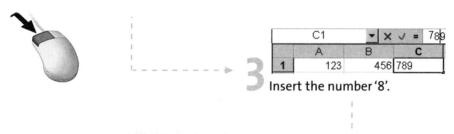

3 Insert the number '8'.

	A	B	C
1	123	456	789
2			

4 Confirm the entry, for example with the Enter key.

Undoing entries

In real life it is usually very difficult to undo things. In Excel this is very easy.

TIP

This button **undoes** the last entry you have made. With every click, one command is undone.

1 Click on the *Undo* button.

	A	B	C
1	123	456	79

2 The last entry has been 'undone'.

Example:

You do not wish to undo only one, but the last four commands.

Next to the button *Undo* there is a downwards pointing arrow. When you click on it, you will see a LIST of operations that can be undone.

1 Activate the LIST.

2 Select the **last four operations**, by dragging downwards **without** pressing the mouse button.
Only when you have marked the last four operations, click with the left mouse button.

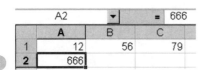

3 If you have followed the instructions correctly, your worksheet will look like this.

When 'undoing' a particular operation, all the **preceding** operations on the list are automatically reversed as well.

You only ever reverse the **last** commands. You cannot reverse individual commands (one here and one there).

Redoing entries

 In connection with the *Undo* button, we need to mention the *Redo* function.

 When you want to carry out a previously undone operation, click on the *Redo* button.

Example:

You wish to carry out the four reversed commands again.

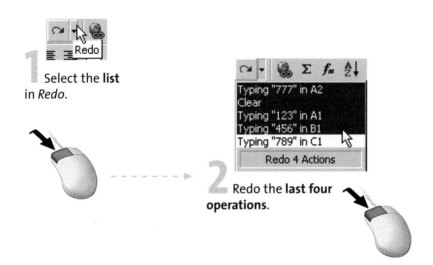

1 Select the **list** in *Redo*.

2 Redo the **last four operations**.

Of course, you can also click on the button once. The next last command is reinstated.

1 Click on the
Redo button.

	A	B	C
1	123	456	789

C1   ▼   =   789

2 You should be back to where
you were before the *Undo* and *Redo*
functions were explained. Are you?

Practise, practise and practise again!

Practice makes perfect (*Excel*lent). To reinforce what you have learnt, please work through the following exercises. The answers can be found in the Appendix. Only one of the answers is correct.

Which command sequence activates ScreenTips?

❏ FORMAT/FONT/SCREENTIPS

❏ VIEW/TOOLBARS/CUSTOMIZE/ *ScreenTips* tab

❏ VIEW/TOOLBARS/CUSTOMIZE/ *Options* tab */Display ScreenTips on toolbars*

How are cell names structured?

❏ First the **cell** and then the **column** is listed.

❏ First the **column** and then the **row** listed.

❏ First the **row** and then the **column** is listed.

What does the mouse pointer look like when it is in an Excel worksheet?

❏   ⊕

❏   I

❏   ↖

3

What's in this chapter?

Let's go! In this chapter you will carry out your first calculations. They will still be pretty basic.

Back to school: you will be taught how to add (+), subtract (-), multiply (*) and divide (/), just like in primary school. Here Excel is used as an advanced calculator. However, the essential advantage of the software is: if you want to insert new numbers, you do not have to repeat the whole calculation.

You merely replace the old number with the new one. Excel automatically recalculates the result.

You already know about:

You are going to learn about:

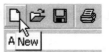

Calculating with numbers

Your time has come. You are going to carry out your first **calculation**.

Example:

You wish to calculate the sum of the numbers '7', '88' and '999'.

The first calculation is a simple addition of three values that are docked one above the other.

> 7
>
> 88
>
> 999

Enter each number into a different cell. Click on the cell, enter the value, and confirm the calculation by pressing the ⏎ key, for example.

	A	B	C
1			
2		✛	
3			

1 Click on cell 'B2'.

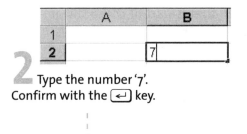

2 Type the number '7'.
Confirm with the ⏎ key.

3 In cell 'B3' enter the number '88'.
Press the ⏎ key.

4 In cell 'B4' enter the number '999'.
Again, confirm with the ⏎ key.

The result

The result of adding the three numbers together is
supposed to appear in cell 'B5'. Important: you need
to enter an **equal sign** (=). In this way you inform
Excel, that a formula is going to follow.

	7
	88
	999
=	

There must always be an equal sign (=) in front
of an operation. In this way the program
knows that what is going to follow is not an
entry but a arithmetical operation.

CAUTION

You need to instruct Excel as
to which cells you want TO
ADD (B2,B3,B4). You can do
this with a mouse-click.

51

7	
88	
999	
=B2+B3+B4	

Click on the first cell that is part of the addition. Then enter the add sign '+'.

Afterwards activate the second cell and again type '+'.

Click on the last cell and confirm the formula, for example with the ⏎ key. Excel displays the result of the operation.

General:

Result = Cell1 + Cell2 + Cell3

In this example:

Cell B5 = Cell B2 + Cell B3 + Cell B4

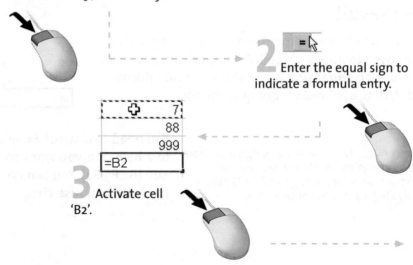

Click on cell 'B5', if necessary.

2 Enter the equal sign to indicate a formula entry.

3 Activate cell 'B2'.

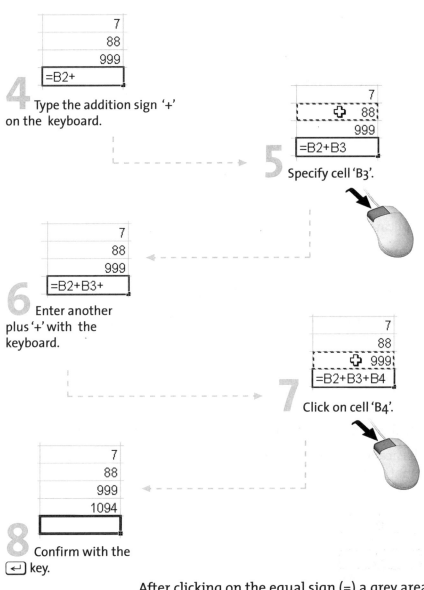

4 Type the addition sign '+' on the keyboard.

5 Specify cell 'B3'.

6 Enter another plus '+' with the keyboard.

7 Click on cell 'B4'.

8 Confirm with the ⏎ key.

After clicking on the equal sign (=) a grey area appears on the screen.

Here you can see the result of the operation while you are entering the formula.

▼ | X ✓ | = | =B2+B3+B4

Formula result = 1094   OK   Cancel

Calculating with Excel

For subtraction, multiplication or division, the procedure is the same as for the addition. Only the respective arithmetical sign changes according to which operation is carried out.

Arithmetic signs in Excel:

Operation	Sign in Excel
Addition	+
Subtraction	-
Multiplication	*
Division	/

Different numbers – new result

The advantage of Excel is that you can subsequently change numbers. You do not have to repeat the whole calculation each time.

Example:

You wish to change the value '7' to '77'.

Delete the number '7', by clicking on the cell and typing '77'.

You basically **overtype** the old value with a new one. The result is automatically recalculated.

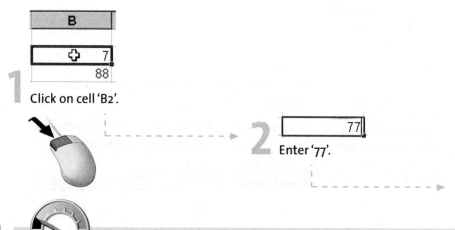

1 Click on cell 'B2'.

2 Enter '77'.

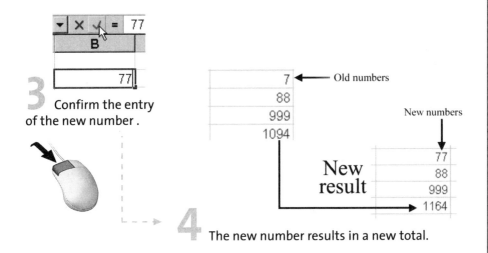

3 Confirm the entry of the new number .

7 ◄─── Old numbers
88
999
1094

New numbers

77
88
999
1164

New result

4 The new number results in a new total.

Using AutoSum

To calculate sums Excel offers a quick command.

Example:

You wish to calculate the sum of the following numbers:

1

22

333

1 Click on cell 'C2'.

1

2 Type the number '1'.
Confirm with the ⏎ key.

55

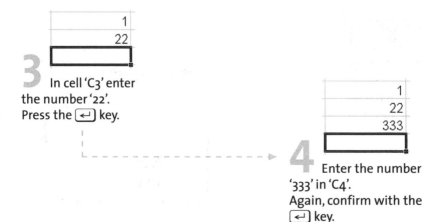

3 In cell 'C3' enter the number '22'. Press the ⏎ key.

4 Enter the number '333' in 'C4'. Again, confirm with the ⏎ key.

For neighbouring cells (on top of or next to each other) Excel provides a shortcut. In this way you do not need to enter '+' after every cell.

Before

Sum = **Cell1 + Cell2 + Cell3**

New

Sum = Sum (**Cell1; Cell2; Cell3**)

Click on the **Sum icon** (*AutoSum* button). Σ

Excel automatically frames the cells with a **dotted line**.

Now Excel displays 'SUM (C2:C4)' in the Formula bar .

Thus, the cells 'C2, C3, C4' are added together.

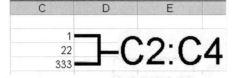

The colon ':' means 'to'.

Excel adds up the numbers in the cells from **'C2' to 'C4'**.

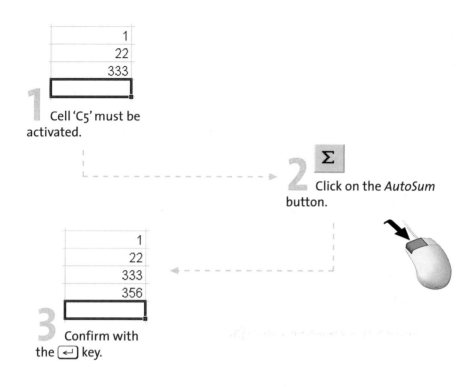

1 Cell 'C5' must be activated.

2 Click on the *AutoSum* button.

3 Confirm with the ⏎ key.

If you want to calculate cells or cell ranges which are not next to each other... press the Ctrl **key** and click with the **mouse**,

or

enter a **semicolon** as a separator after selecting each cell.

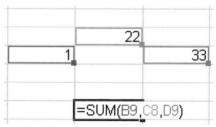

57

Entering text

The 'little' calculation still looks a little 'bare', that is why you want to label it. Entering text (letters) differs quite considerably from entering numbers.

Of course, Excel can only calculate with numbers and not with text.

	A	B	C	D
1				
2		77	1	
3		88	22	
4		999	333	
5		1164	356	
6				

123	456	789
345	1	0,5
678	77	4711

In **cells**, numbers **are always** right-aligned .

On the other hand, text is **always** left-aligned **in cells**.

Text	Excel	XYZ
Football	EASY	Discount
Profit	ABC	Turnover

Watch out for combinations: numbers, letters, and signs!

Excel does not recognise a value such as '123.—' as a number. It perceives the expression as text because of the characters '—'. Thus the entry would be left-aligned.

34°	£12	17.5% VAT	10 pence
12"	5,- euro	3% Discount	20 guilders
5, -	£7	10 dollar	1 litre
5 kg	10 m	1 cm	10 m2/sqm
12	E611	A1	56 Plus

Here you can see other combination entries, which are **not** seen as **numbers** but as text by Excel.

In cells, Excel distinguishes
between numbers (right-aligned,
text (left-aligned) and formulas
(equal sign).

	A	B	C
1	✛		
2		77	1
3		88	22
4		999	333
5		1164	356

1 Click on cell 'A1'.

	A	B	C
1	Sum		
2		77	1
3		88	22
4		999	333
5		1164	356

2 Type the word 'Sum'.

	A	B	C
1	Sum		
2		77	1
3		88	22
4		999	333
5	✛	1164	356

3 Click on cell 'A5'.

	A	B	C
1	Sum		
2		77	1
3		88	22
4		999	333
5	Total	1164	356

4 Enter the word 'Total:'.
Press the ⏎ key.

Workshop: calculating VAT

The following workshop contains everything you have learnt so far in this chapter: you will enter text and numbers, multiply, and add up cells.

Example:

You wish to calculate the tax (currently 17.5 % VAT = Value Added Tax on the net amount of '200' and the total gross amount .

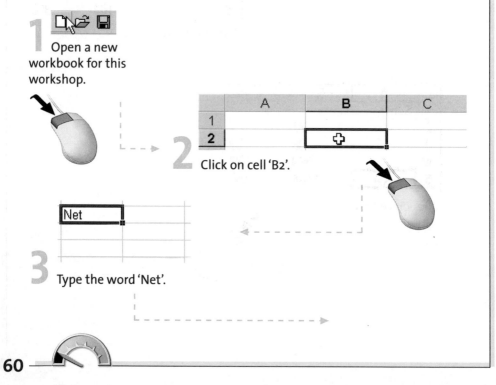

1 Open a new workbook for this workshop.

2 Click on cell 'B2'.

3 Type the word 'Net'.

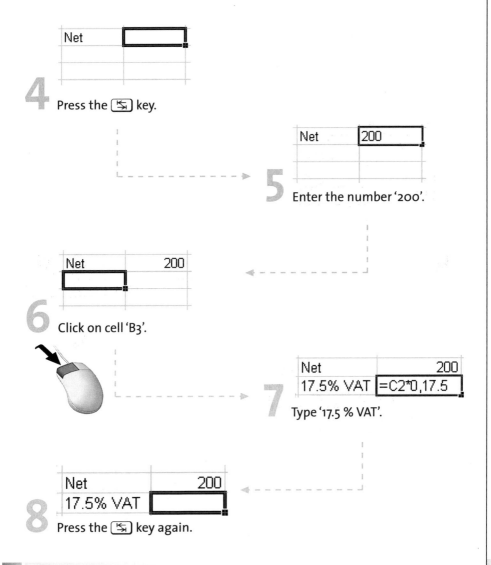

Net

4 Press the ⑤ key.

Net　200

5 Enter the number '200'.

Net　200

6 Click on cell 'B3'.

Net　200
17.5% VAT　=C2*0,17.5

7 Type '17.5 % VAT'.

Net　200
17.5% VAT

8 Press the ⑤ key again.

If you want to enter arithmetical signs such as '=,+,-' as text, you need to use the apostrophe (') before typing them.

61

Now the calculation of the tax amount.

How much is 17.5 % of 200?

Enter the formula: '200 * 0.175' (the cell 'C2 * 0.175')

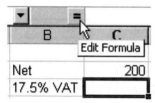

1 Enter the equal sign to indicate a formula entry.

Net	✛ 200
17.5% VAT	=C2

2 Click on cell 'C2'.

Net	200
17.5% VAT	=C2*

3 On your keyboard type the character * for **multiplication**.

Net	200
17.5% VAT	=C2*0.16

4 Enter '0.175'.

?	Formula result = 35		OK
2	Net	200	
3	17.5% VAT	=C2*0.175	

5 Confirm the completion of the calculation with the OK button.

After you have calculated the tax amount, you want to find out the gross amount (that is: net amount + tax amount).

Σ For this you use the Sum icon (*AutoSum* button).

Net	200
17.5% VAT	35
Gross|	

1 Click on cell 'B4' and enter the word 'Gross' for the gross amount.

Net	200
17.5% VAT	35
Gross	

2 Press the Tab key.

3 Activate the *AutoSum* button.

Net	200
17.5% VAT	35
Gross	235

4 Confirm with the Enter key.

Net	200
17.5% VAT	32
Gross	232

5 The result of the calculation: '235'.

If you now change the net amount, you will get the appropriate tax and gross amount.

Example:

The net amount '200' is replaced by '500'.

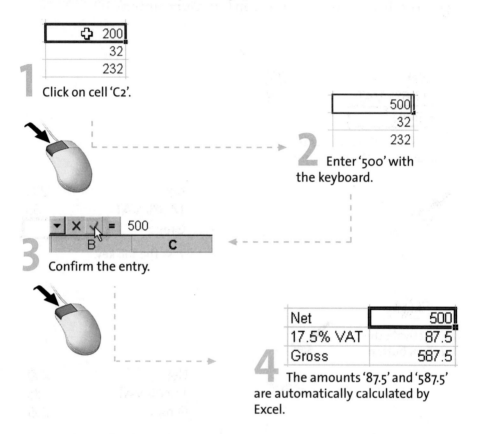

1 Click on cell 'C2'.

2 Enter '500' with the keyboard.

3 Confirm the entry.

4 The amounts '87.5' and '587.5' are automatically calculated by Excel.

Enter the net amounts '600, 750, 900' respectively, and observe how the cells are modified by the new entry.

Practise, practise and practise again!

Practice makes perfect (*Exce*lent)! Again, you can find the answers in the relevant Appendix. Several answers are possible!

I. Exercise

Which sign do you need to enter in front of a calculation?

❏   =

❏   None

❏   '

II. Exercise

Which signs are used for the various arithmetical operations in Excel?

- + * / \ x X

Division: ...

Addition: ...

Multiplication: ...

Subtraction: ...

III. Exercise

C2:C4 – The sign ':' means:

❏   C2 to C4

❏   C2 divided by cell C4

❏   C2 or C4

❏   The cell range C2 to C4

IV. Exercise

If necessary, create a new workbook.

A 'new workbook' means that you have a new set of unedited 'worksheets'.

Solve the following problems with the help of Excel:

22 + 34	33 × 44	546 : 77	75 + 98	159 - 89
45 × 78	45 × 56	188 + 78	78 + 99	145 - 99

V. Exercise

When does Excel recognise the entry as a number and when as text?

Try it out!

234,56	75,-- pounds	ABC
23 dollars	- 34	0,34
34 °	75,--	-,35
+ 78	4711	0815

VI. Exercise

 If necessary, open a new workbook. Enter the correct formulas into the cells.

Amount	500
Discount 10 %	50
Result	450

	A	B	C
1			
2			
3		Amount	500
4		Discount 10%	???
5		Total	450
6			

Change the amount to '600, 700, 900'

CAUTION

Exit Excel
without saving.

67

4

What's in this chapter?

Do you often wonder, like the author of this book, where all your money has gone by the end of the month? Surely, you had some money at the beginning of the month. Have you run out of money again? Left too much in the pub? And you wanted to go to Florida for your next holiday. Well, Cornwall is nice too and can be very interesting.

If you occasionally lose track of your pound notes and coins, Excel can help you organise your finances.

You already know about:

You are going to learn about:

Adjusting column widths

If an entry is too long for a cell, Excel will accept it anyway.

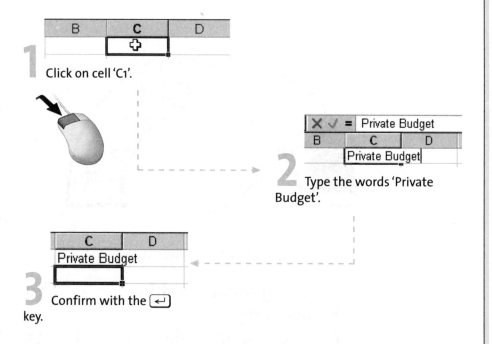

1 Click on cell 'C1'.

2 Type the words 'Private Budget'.

3 Confirm with the ⏎ key.

There is not enough space in the cell for the expression 'Private Budget'. The column is too narrow.

Words or text might be even longer than 'Private Budget of the Flintstones in December'. You can see the **contents of a cell** on the **Formula bar**.

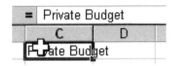

1 Click on the cell 'C1' and look at its contents in the Formula bar.

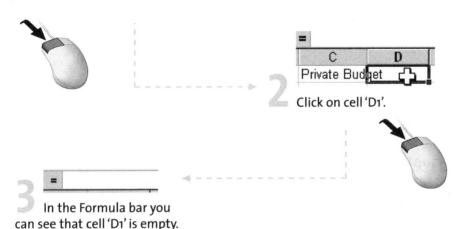

2 Click on cell 'D1'.

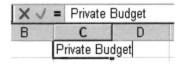

3 In the Formula bar you can see that cell 'D1' is empty.

To improve clarity you can adjust the **column width**. Move the mouse pointer between two column headings. It changes its appearance.

Holding down the mouse button, you can adjust the **column width** until it is the right size. Then release the mouse button.

However, there is an even easier option!

CAUTION

When you double-click on the line between two columns, Excel automatically **adjusts** the column width to accommodate the **longest expression** (number or text).

71

1 C ⊹ D

Place the mouse pointer exactly between columns 'C' and 'D'.

C
Private Budget

2 Double-click with the left mouse button.

Highlighting text

Private Budget In Excel you can highlight individual words (or numbers). This procedure is called **formatting**.

All the tools you need are to be found on the **Formatting toolbar**.

Characters can be highlighted by formatting them using *Bold*, *Underline*, and so on.

Arial		Font		
		Font Size	10	
	B	**Bold**		
		Italic	*I*	
	U	Underline		

For example, you can modify the font and font size or highlight text by making it **Bold** or *Italic*.

1
C
Private Budget

Click on cell 'C1'.

2
B *I* U

Activate *Bold*.

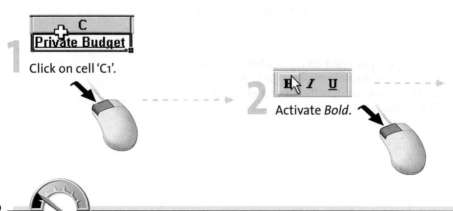

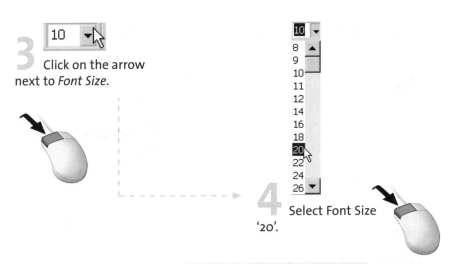

3 Click on the arrow next to *Font Size*.

4 Select Font Size '20'.

The FORMAT/CELLS menu option offers an additional option. On the *Font* tab you have additional options. You may choose *Superscript* or *Subscript*.

You can also select *Double Underline*. Any future printout will show the chosen highlights.

The **Preview window** is particularly interesting. Here you can check what the chosen formatting looks like before you confirm it with the *OK* button.

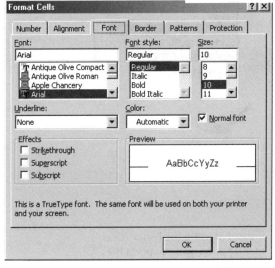

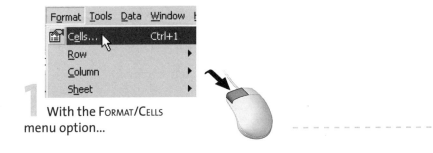

1 With the FORMAT/CELLS menu option...

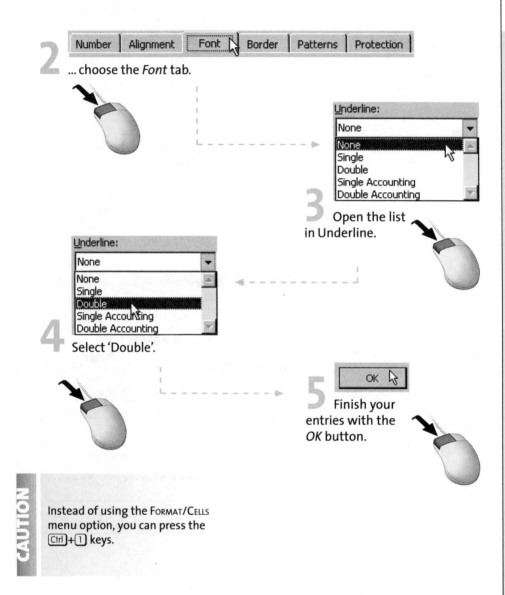

2 ... choose the *Font* tab.

3 Open the list in Underline.

4 Select 'Double'.

5 Finish your entries with the *OK* button.

As you have increased the font size and thus the cell contents, you will need to adjust the column width again.

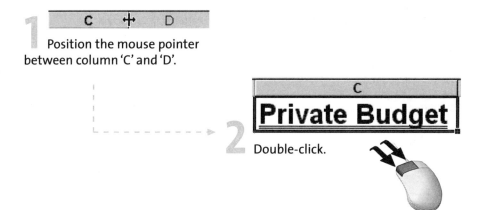

1 Position the mouse pointer between column 'C' and 'D'.

2 Double-click.

Moving around on the worksheet

As in this example, you may need to enter data at the very bottom of your screen.

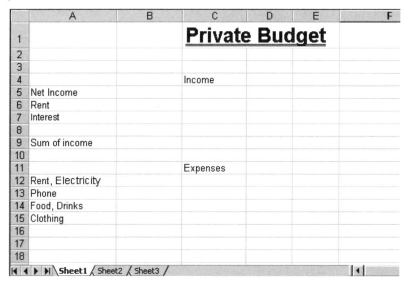

The entries even go beyond it. Row '16' is still visible in this position.

However, what about the rows which follow? Of course the sheet does not end here: in total there are exactly 65.536 (!) rows.

To scroll more quickly
through a worksheet,
use the **scroll bar** at
the right margin of
the screen.

You only ever see an **extract** on your screen.
You just **scroll** through it.

To continue your entries you can use the
cursor keys, in this case ⬇.

	A	B	C
4			Income
5	Net Income		
6	Rent		
7	Interest		
8			
9	Sum of income		
10			
11			Expenses
12	Rent, Electricity		
13	Phone		
14	Food, Drinks		
15	Clothing		

1 Enter the following data in the appropriate
cells.

2 Holding down
the left mouse button
scroll...

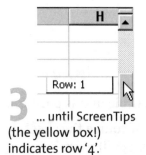

3 ... until ScreenTips
(the yellow box!)
indicates row '4'.

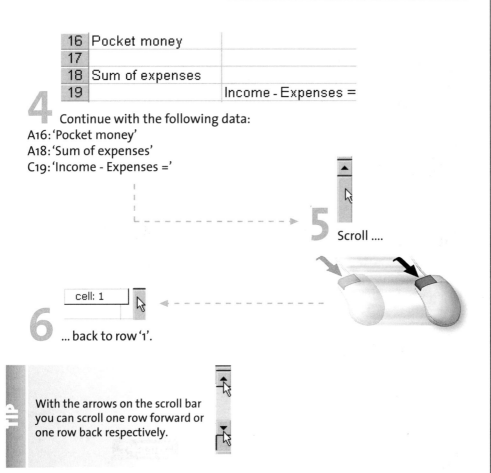

4 Continue with the following data:
A16: 'Pocket money'
A18: 'Sum of expenses'
C19: 'Income - Expenses ='

5 Scroll ....

6 ... back to row '1'.

TIP

With the arrows on the scroll bar you can scroll one row forward or one row back respectively.

What is the 'brush' for?

You know how to highlight text and numbers. If you want to apply an existing formatting several times, it is best to use the *Format Painter* button .

When you click on it once, the mouse pointer turns into a brush as soon as you drag it onto the **worksheet**.

77

1 Click on cell 'C4'.

2 Activate *Bold*.

3 Switch on the *Format Painter* button by clicking on the button.

4 Select cell 'C11'.

5 The **Bold** formatting has been applied.

With a single click on the button you can only format once. However, when you double-click on the 'brush', you can use it as often as you want.

Format Painter button	Effect
Single click	You can apply the **formatting** once.
Double click	You can apply the **formatting any number of times**.
Pressing the Esc key or clicking on the *Format Painter* button again	The function has been switched off.

1 Click on cell 'C11', if necessary.

2 Switch on the function with a double click.

	A	B
4		
5	Net Income	
6	Rent	
7	Interest	
8		
9	Total Income	

3 Activate cell 'A9'.

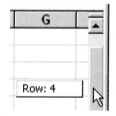

4 Scroll until ScreenTips displays 'Row: 4'.

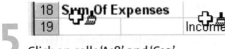

5

Click on cells 'A18' and 'C19'.

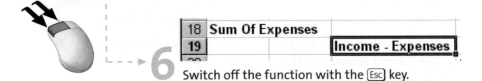

6

Switch off the function with the [Esc] key.

7

A ✛ B

Move the mouse pointer between the column headings 'A' and 'B'.

	A
1	
2	
3	
4	
5	Net Income
6	Rent
7	Interest
8	
9	**Total Income**

8

Adjust the width of column 'A'. If necessary scroll back to row '1'.

Calculating sums

To calculate numbers, there is another quick command.

You can use the *AutoSum* button. (See **Chapter 3.**)

Income	
	5000
Σ	1000
	50

Excel frames all cells that contain numbers, up to a cell which contains text, with a **dotted line**.

	income	
Net Income		5000
Rent		1000
Interest		50

1 Enter the values for income into cells 'C5, C6, C7' and ...

	Expenses	
Rent, Electricity		1600
Phone		450
Food, Drink		200
Clothing		1000
Pocket money		200

2 ... for expenses into cells 'C12' to 'C16'.

5000
1000
50

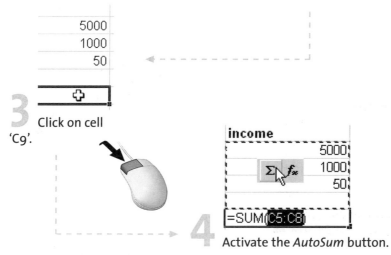

3 Click on cell 'C9'.

income	
	5000
∑ *fx*	1000
	50
=SUM(C5:C8)	

4 Activate the *AutoSum* button.

If there is an **empty cell** between the numbers and the result, it will also be framed. As empty cells do not contain values, this does not affect the calculation .

You see that Excel displays 'SUM (C5:C8)'. Thus the cells 'C5, C6, C7' and the empty cell 'C8' are added together.

Income	
	5000
	1000
	50
=SUM(C5:C8)	

C	
income	
	5000
	1000
	50
	6050

1 Confirm with the ⏎ key.

G	
Row: 4	

2 Scroll until ScreenTips displays 'Row: 4'.

Expenses	
	1600
	450
	200
	1000
	200
	🕂

3 Click on cell 'C18' ...

4 ... and then on the *AutoSum* button.

Expenses	
	1600
	450
	200
	1000
	200
	3450

5 Confirm with the ⏎ key.

Do you want to know how much is left? To find out you need the sum of your income minus your expenses.

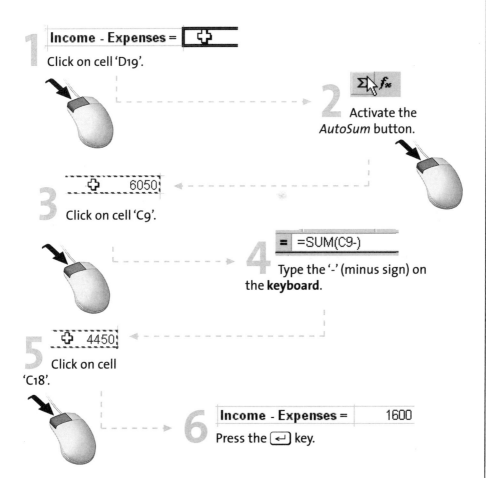

1 Income - Expenses = ⊹

Click on cell 'D19'.

2 Activate the *AutoSum* button.

3 ⊹ 6050

Click on cell 'C9'.

4 = =SUM(C9-)

Type the '-' (minus sign) on the **keyboard**.

5 ⊹ 4450

Click on cell 'C18'.

6 Income - Expenses = 1600

Press the ⏎ key.

Moving cells

WHAT'S THIS?

Drag and drop - allows you to move **cell contents**.

You wish to move the cells or their contents 'C19' ('Income - Expenses') and 'D19' ('1500') to improve the look of the sheet.

You do not need to enter all the values again, simply use the **drag and drop** method.

How to drag and drop

Crucial for the successful execution of the drag and drop method is the **appearance** of the **mouse pointer**. It indicates which functions are currently available to you.

On the worksheet the mouse pointer usually appears as a white cross. With this – as you already know – you click on cells.

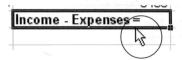

However, when you position the mouse pointer on the **outline** of the cell highlight, the pointer turns into an **arrow**.

TIP

You can only use the drag and drop method only when the mouse pointer has the shape of an arrow on the worksheet.

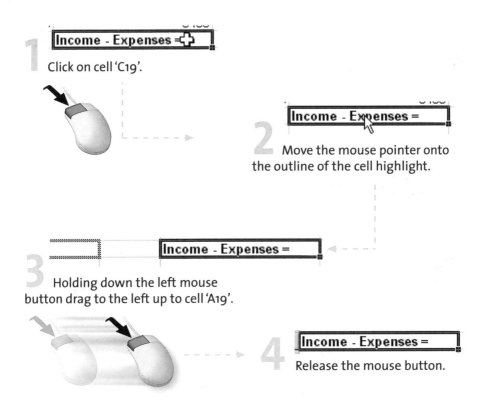

1 Click on cell 'C19'.

2 Move the mouse pointer onto the outline of the cell highlight.

3 Holding down the left mouse button drag to the left up to cell 'A19'.

4 Release the mouse button.

As a beginner, if you have difficulties with the drag and drop method, there is an alternative.

Instead of drag and drop you can use the button with the **scissors** (=*Cut*)! When you cut something, the original disappears, and can be inserted at a different place.

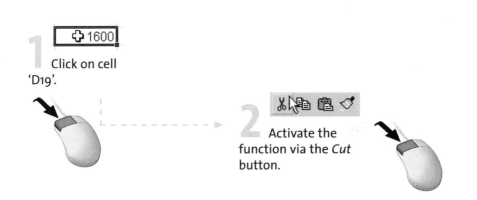

1 Click on cell 'D19'.

2 Activate the function via the *Cut* button.

85

The result: Excel frames the cell with a dotted line.

 What next? First you specify with a mouse click where – that is in which cell – you wish the data to be located.

Then click on the *Insert* button.

> 1600

4450

⊕   1600

1 Specify cell 'C19'.

2 Activate the *Paste* button.

4450

1600

3 The contents have been moved from cell 'D19' to cell 'C19'.

Deleting or inserting columns

Column 'B' is now empty in this worksheet. It can be deleted. To delete it, the keyboard shortcut Ctrl + - is used.

⊕B

1 Click on the column heading 'B'.

B

2 First press the (Ctrl) key, keep holding it down, and then also press the (-) key.

A	B
Rent	1000
Interest	50
Total Income	6050
	Expenses
Rent, Electricity	1600
Phone	450
Food, Drink	200
Clothing	1000

3 The empty column has disappeared.

B	C
5000	
1000	
50	
6050	
Expenses	
1600	
450	

4 Remove the marking with a mouse click.

Of course, you can also insert cells, instead of deleting them. To insert cells, press the keyboard shortcut (Ctrl)+(+) or select the INSERT/COLUMNS menu option.

87

Keyboard shortcut	Menu option	Effects
Ctrl + +	INSERT/COLUMNS	Inserts columns
Ctrl + -	EDIT/DELETE CELLS/ COLUMN	Deletes columns

Inserting or deleting rows

You can do the same – inserting or deleting– with rows.

Click on the row heading '19'.

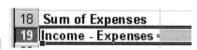
First press the Ctrl key, keep pressing it, and then also press the + key.

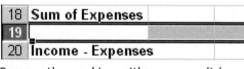
The result: a row has been inserted.

Remove the marking with a mouse-click.

Keyboard shortcut	Menu option	Effects
Ctrl + +	INSERT/ROWS	Inserts a row
Ctrl + -	EDIT/DELETE CELLS/ROW	Deletes a row

CAUTION

Do not exit Excel this time! In the next chapter you will learn how to print and save. It is best if you use this worksheet for this purpose.

What's in this chapter?

Do you intend to carry on with your work tomorrow, the day after tomorrow, next year, that is in the next millennium? Would you leave the PC switched on all the time in order to do so? If so, your electricity supplier would surely be the happiest man in the world.

In this chapter you will learn about storing your worksheets on your computer and on diskette.

Private Budget

	5000
Income	1000
	50
	6050

You can print out your worksheet in order to have it on paper, in black and white. However, before you do so, you should check the outcome of the printing process in a preview, in case you need to amend it. This may save paper.

You already know about:

You are going to learn about:

Saving worksheets

Surely you want to store your work on your computer so that you can continue with it at a later date.

The Title bar

The Title bar displays the **workbook** that you are currently editing.

A workbook is like a ring binder which is used to file single sheets. In Excel 2000 you work with sheets, too, which are called worksheets.

You can label and file a ring binder with all the relevant sheets. In Excel this is done by SAVING the workbook.

The word BOOK on the Title bar means that the current workbook has not yet been saved. Thus, it is a name which is automatically assigned by Excel.

The number 1 after the word 'workbook' tells you that you are editing your FIRST workbook on the screen.

An example from the office world:

Office world	Terms in Excel
Ring binder	Workbook
A sheet in a ring binder	Worksheet
An unlabelled ring binder	Not saved, the term 'Book' has been assigned
A labelled ring binder	Saved, a name has been assigned

Storing worksheets on your computer

Do you still have the 'Budget' from Chapter 4?

Private Budget

Income	
Net Income	5000
Rent	1000
Interest	50
Sum of income	6050
Expenses	
Rent, Electricity	1600
Phone	450

If not, just enter anything you like in a cell.

To store a worksheet permanently on your computer's hard disk, you need to **save** the workbook.

An example will make this easier to understand:

What you would usually do in an office	What you do in Excel
Labelling the file 'Spreadsheet'	Assigning a filename
Putting the file into the filing cabinet	Specifying the file location
Closing the filing cabinet	Exiting Excel

To **save**, you can click on the button with the diskette symbol or call up the FILE/SAVE menu option.

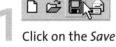

1 Click on the *Save* button.

Save As

Save in: 🗁 My Documents ▼

2 The dialog box opens.

Under *File Name* you specify under which **name** the workbook is to be filed (= labelling a ring binder).

Excel automatically suggests the name 'Book1.xls'. The ending, which is called the extension, '**.xls**' represents the software **Excel**. It is assigned by the program and will not need to be entered in the future.

File name: Book1.xls

1 File name: B|

Type ...

2 File name: Budget|

... the filename 'Budget'.

File name: Book1.xls

In *Save in* you specify **where** you want to file the workbook. Excel automatically suggests 'My Documents'. However, you can specify any other **location**.

Click on the *Save* button.

Private Budget

	Income	
Net Income		5000
Rent		1000
Interest		50
Sum of income		6050

You return to the workbook.

Look at the very top of your screen! In the Title bar you will notice the name 'Budget.xls'.

Microsoft Excel - Budget.xls

The corresponding details are now located in this workbook.

In the *Save As* dialog box, you will find further information.

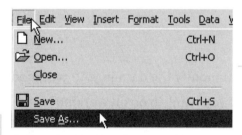

Call up the FILE/SAVE As menu command.

Budget.xls

Activate the workbook 'Budget' with a single mouse-click.

95

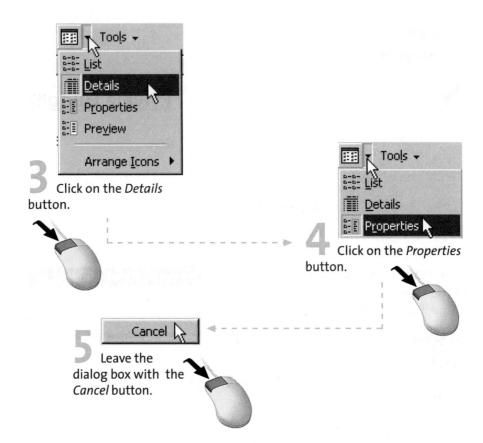

3 Click on the *Details* button.

4 Click on the *Properties* button.

5 Leave the dialog box with the *Cancel* button.

Saving changes

And so, what happens when you modify the data in your workbook?

 When you exit Excel, the program asks you whether you wish to save the changes.

If you want to go on working with Excel, one click on the *Save* button will be enough.

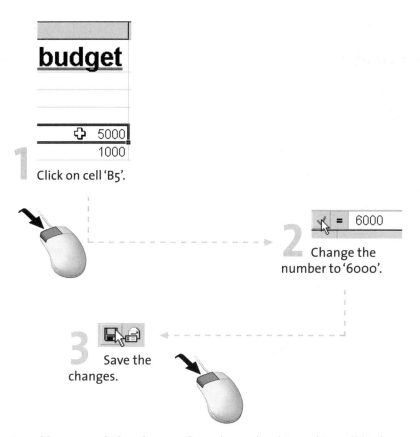

budget

1 Click on cell 'B5'.

2 Change the number to '6000'.

3 Save the changes.

Excel has saved the change from '5000' to '6000' in cell 'B5'.

To Save or to Save As ... ?

... that is the question. What is the difference between *Save* and the FILE/SAVE AS menu command...

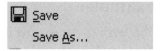

Save

When you make changes to a worksheet in a workbook and subsequently save it, the original data have disappeared or new data have been added.

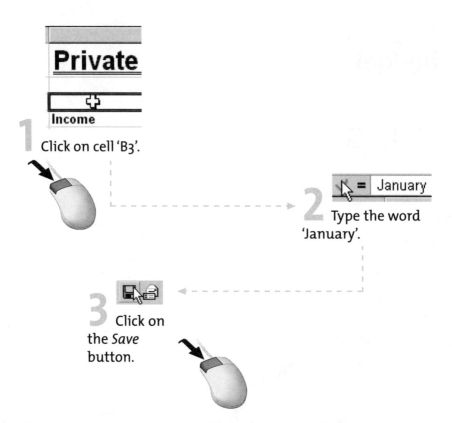

1 Click on cell 'B3'.

2 Type the word 'January'.

3 Click on the *Save* button.

The change is now permanently in the workbook 'Budget'. However, what is the purpose of the FILE/SAVE As menu option... ?

Save As ...

Example:

You wish to draw up a budget for February, too. You want to keep the first worksheet, and save the second separately.

(To make it easier: the values on the worksheet have not been changed!)

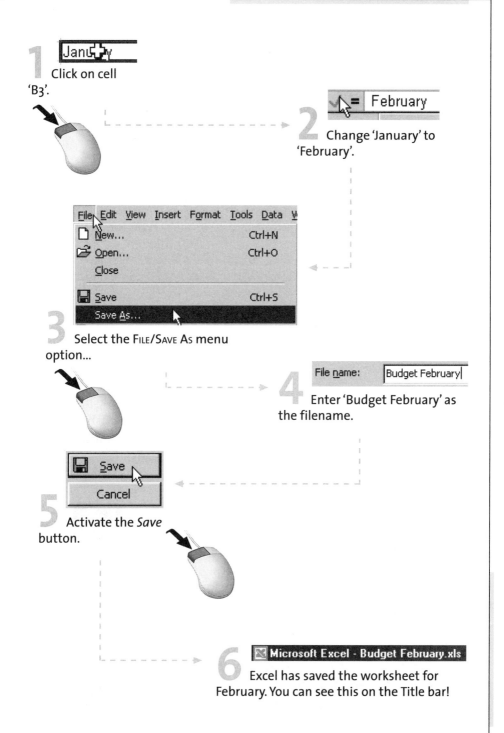

January

1 Click on cell
'B3'.

✓ =	February

2 Change 'January' to
'February'.

File | Edit | View | Insert | Format | Tools | Data | W

☐ New...   Ctrl+N
☞ Open...   Ctrl+O
   Close

🖫 Save   Ctrl+S
   Save As...

3 Select the FILE/SAVE AS menu
option...

File name: Budget February

4 Enter 'Budget February' as
the filename.

🖫 Save
   Cancel

5 Activate the *Save*
button.

Microsoft Excel - Budget February.xls

6 Excel has saved the worksheet for
February. You can see this on the Title bar!

99

Instead of selecting the FILE/SAVE AS menu option... you can press the F12 key. This is an alternative way of opening the *Save As* dialog box.

The above worksheets are stored on your computer's hard disk .

As a rule, the hard disk is a built in memory device which allows storage of large amounts of data. The data is kept even when the computer is switched off.

Saving on diskette

Diskettes can record data by means of a disk drive, permanently store data and when needed can be read again by different computers.

Occasionally you may want to or may need to save a worksheet on diskette, because you wish to use the file on a different computer or for security reasons.

The usual diskette size is 3.5". The front is always labelled. Diskettes have a write-protection option. When the small black switch on the back is in the upper position, the diskette can only be read but cannot be written to.

As in this example, you wish to save your worksheet on diskette, therefore leave the switch in the lower position.

On the front you can see an arrow. Following its direction, insert the diskette into the floppy disk drive of your computer.

Never force a diskette into a disk drive!

1 Insert the diskette into the floppy disk drive of your computer until it 'clicks into place'.

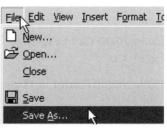

2 Select the FILE/SAVE AS menu option.

TIP

On most computers, the floppy disk drive is referred to as 'A:'.

File name: | Budget February on diskette|

3 Enter the text 'Budget February on diskette' as the filename.

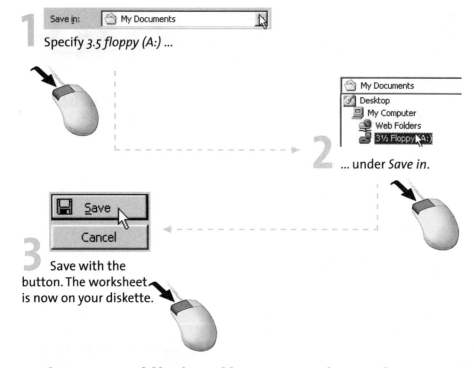

Save in: My Documents

1 Specify *3.5 floppy (A:)* ...

My Documents
Desktop
My Computer
Web Folders
3½ Floppy (A:)

2 ... under *Save in*.

Save

Cancel

3 Save with the button. The worksheet is now on your diskette.

Excel 2000 can read files from older versions such as Excel 97 or Excel 5.0.

However, an older version cannot read Excel 2000 data!

Save as type: Microsoft Excel Workbook (*.xls)

Microsoft Excel Workbook (*.xls)
Web Page (*.htm; *.html)
Template (*.xlt)
Text (Tab delimited) (*.txt)
Unicode Text (*.txt)
Microsoft Excel 5.0/95 Workbook (*.xls)

Printing worksheets

Before you print out a worksheet, you should first check it for errors on your screen.

The Page Break Preview

Excel displays the data to be printed on each page and **how many pages** the printed spreadsheet will consist of.

Under the VIEW/PAGE BREAK PREVIEW menu option a worksheet is shown as the actual **printed pages**. Here you can also carry out modifications.

1 In the VIEW menu select ...

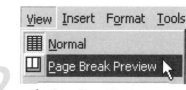

2 ... the PAGE BREAK PREVIEW command.

This is up to you! To suppress the dialog box in future, click on the check box and confirm with the *OK* button.

Welcome to Page Break Preview

You can adjust the page breaks by clicking and dragging them with your mouse.

☐ Do not show this balloon again

[OK]

If you want the message to be displayed again, simply click on the *OK* button.

OK

	Private Budget	
	Income	
Net Income		6000
Rent		1000
Interest		50
Sum of income		7050
	Expenses	
Rent, Elecricity		1600
Phone		450
Food, Drinks		1200
Clothing		1000
Pocket money		200
Sum of expenses		4450
Income - Expenses		2600

1 The worksheet in this example fits on one page.

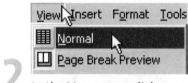

2 In the VIEW menu click on the NORMAL command.

The Print Preview

Before you print your worksheet you should check it with Print Preview, because you might want to change something in the way it looks.

 You can find the *Print Preview* command in the FILE menu. However, it is much quicker using the button on the Standard toolbar.

One click and you are in **Print Preview** mode, that is, you can see a preview of the actual print-out.

Zoom   With the *Zoom* button you can enlarge and reduce the **view** of the worksheet. The future print-out is not affected by this.

By pressing the Esc key or with the *Close* button, you return to the original worksheet in your current workbook.

1 Click on the *Print Preview* button.

2 Operate the *Zoom* button to enlarge or reduce the view.

Zoom

Private Budget

	Income	
Net Income		6000
Rent		1000
Interest		50
Sum of income		**7050**
	Expenses	
Rent, Elecricity		1600
Phone		450
Food, Drinks		1200
Clothing		1000
Pocket money		200
Sum of expenses		4450
Income - Expenses		**2600**

3 You see the preview of the actual print-out.

Close   Help

4 Return to the workbook with the Esc key or the *Close* button.

Printing out worksheets

When you choose the *Print* button, you are able to print your worksheet in black and white.

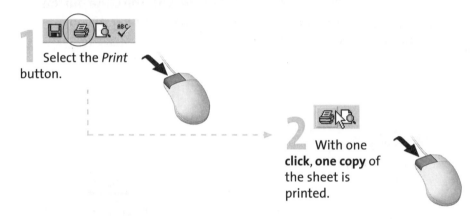

1 Select the *Print* button.

2 With one **click**, **one copy** of the sheet is printed.

You can also use the FILE/PRINT menu command to send to print.

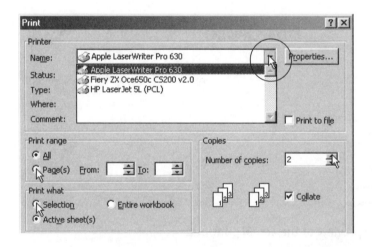

Here you can specify further details. Thus, you can define **the number of copies** that you wish to print , or which printer you want to use, if, for example, you have a black and white as well as a colour printer.

The 'Full Screen' view

Occasionally, the screen details in Excel are not sufficiently clear. One option to improve this is the FULL SCREEN view . You can find the command in the VIEW menu.

Activating the command enlarges the screen detail of the worksheet. The toolbars disappear from the screen. Only the Menu bar remains.

You EXIT the 'Full Screen' view, by selecting the VIEW/FULL SCREEN again.

In the FULL SCREEN view you can activate the toolbars by right-clicking on the menu. Then just click on the toolbars.

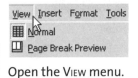

1 Open the VIEW menu.

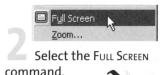

2 Select the FULL SCREEN command.

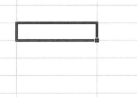

Activating/deactivating the gridlines

If the gridlines in Excel bother you, you can hide them. They are not printed anyway. But, after all, there are people who do not like to be behind bars.

107

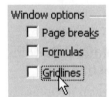

When you deactivate the gridlines, the worksheet appears as a clean empty area. You cannot see the cells, but they are still there. You can continue working 'as usual' on your worksheet.

Select the TOOLS/OPTIONS menu command and activate the *View* tab. Under *Window options* deactivate the gridlines. In the same way, you can activate them again.

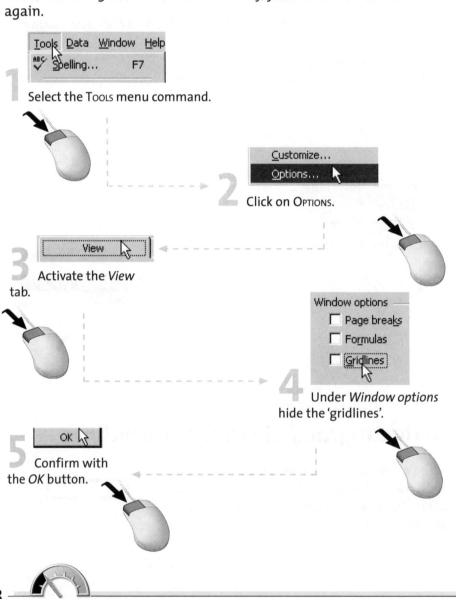

1 Select the TOOLS menu command.

2 Click on OPTIONS.

3 Activate the *View* tab.

4 Under *Window options* hide the 'gridlines'.

5 Confirm with the *OK* button.

The worksheet looks slightly unfamiliar without the gridlines. However, it does not restrict the handling of the program. You can execute everything you have learnt/are going to learn in this book as usual.

For Excel beginners, it is surely easier to work with the **gridlines**.

You will need to make up your own mind as to whether you prefer to work with or without gridlines!

And back again!

To make sure that we can carry on working properly in the next chapters, it is recommended that you deactivate the 'Full Screen', and activate the gridlines again. (If you have not already done so.)

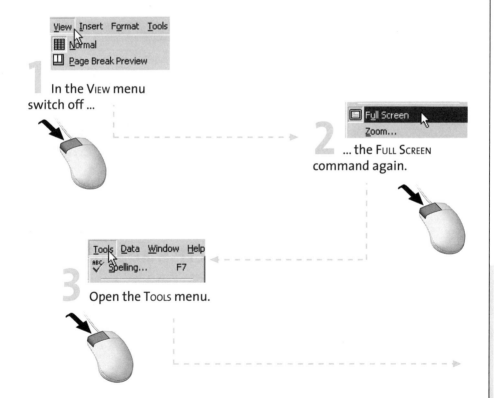

1 In the VIEW menu switch off ...

2 ... the FULL SCREEN command again.

3 Open the TOOLS menu.

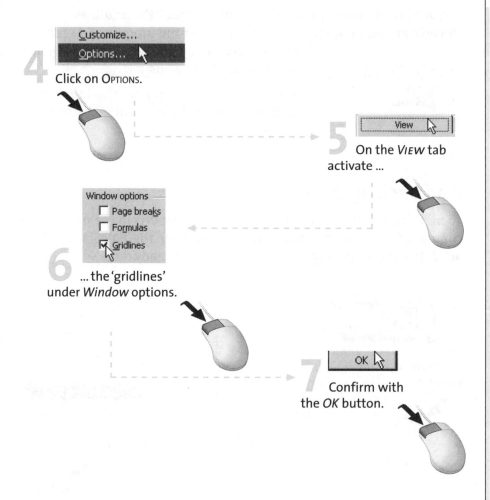

4 Click on OPTIONS.

5 On the *VIEW* tab activate ...

6 ... the 'gridlines' under *Window* options.

7 Confirm with the *OK* button.

Practise, practise and practise again!

1 Create a new workbook for this exercise.

	A	B
1	**Private Budget**	
2		
3	**Expenses**	1200
4	Flat (Rent)	350
5	Electricity and Gas	250
6	Mortgage	150
7	Insurance	80
8	Sports Club	400
9	Food	40
10	Dog Food	400
11	Clothing	250
12	Car	200
13	Miscellaneous	???
14	Sum of Expenses	
15		
16	**Income**	
17	Net income	5000
18	Extra Income	400
19	Sum of Income	???
20		
21	**Income Surplus**	???

2 Create the worksheet as shown. Adjust the width of column 'A'. Enter the appropriate formulas into the corresponding cells. (The answers can be found in the Appendix.)

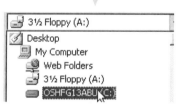

3 In the *Save As* dialog box under *Save in* enter drive 'C' and ...

TIP

Exit Excel! The worksheets in your workbook have been saved. In the next chapter you will learn how to access saved worksheets again.

4 ...'My Documents'. **Save** the workbook under the name 'Exercise'.

CAUTION

If you are going to switch off your PC, do not forget to remove the diskette you have used in this chapter from your floppy disk drive.

What's in this chapter?

Do you want to continue with yesterday's, last week's, last year's work today? In the last chapter you learnt how to store – save – the worksheets in your workbook. How do you get them back onto your screen? This chapter tells you how to access – open – existing workbooks.

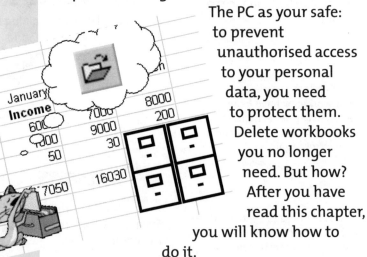

The PC as your safe: to prevent unauthorised access to your personal data, you need to protect them. Delete workbooks you no longer need. But how? After you have read this chapter, you will know how to do it.

You already know about:

You are going to learn about:

Accessing workbooks

Open an existing workbook in Excel, this must have been saved first (as outlined in Chapter 5).

After saving it, you may have exited the program and a few hours or days have passed.

Now you have restarted Excel and wish to continue working with a saved workbook.

To make it easier to understand, consider this example:

General office practice	Excel
Opening a filing cabinet	Starting Excel
Opening the file 'spreadsheet'	Opening the workbook 'spreadsheet'

You have, therefore, already opened the filing cabinet (you have started Excel) and now you only need to take your workbook out.

In Excel, click on the *Open* button or select the FILE/OPEN menu option . In both cases you will open the same dialog box.

Example:

You wish to open the workbook 'Budget February from the diskette', which you have saved on diskette in the last chapter.

Under *Look in* you specify **where** you have saved your workbook. If it is located on a **diskette**, click on '3.5 floppy (A:)'.

1 Insert the diskette you have used in the last chapter into the floppy disk drive of your computer.

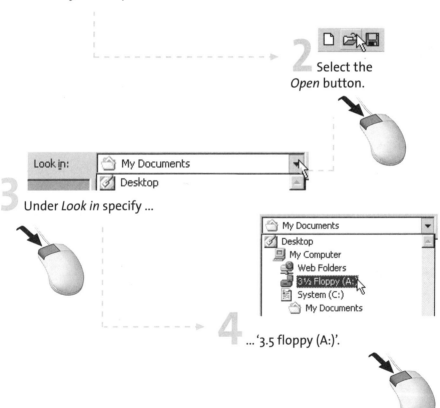

2 Select the *Open* button.

| Look in: | 📁 My Documents ▼ |
| | 📁 Desktop |

3 Under *Look in* specify ...

| 📁 My Documents ▼ |
| 📁 Desktop |
| 🖥 My Computer |
| 🌐 Web Folders |
| 💾 3½ Floppy (A:) |
| 📁 System (C:) |
| 📁 My Documents |

4 ... '3.5 floppy (A:)'.

Finally, enter the filename of the workbook that you wish to open. In this case it is: 'Budget February on diskette.xls'.

Either double-click on the **filename** or mark it with a single click and confirm with the *Open* button. Both methods take you back to the screen: the selected workbook opens.

Double-click on the name *Budget February on diskette*.

The workbook appears on the screen.

Of course, you can also open workbooks that are stored on the **hard disk** of your computer.

Example:

You wish to open the workbook 'Budget February', which you have saved on the hard disk in the last chapter.

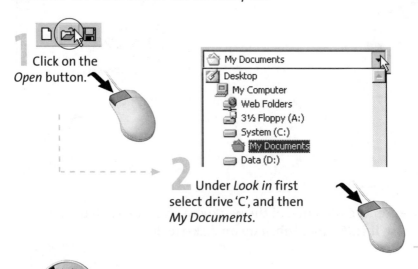
Click on the *Open* button.

Under *Look in* first select drive 'C', and then *My Documents*.

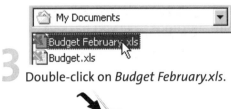

3 Double-click on *Budget February.xls*.

The recently used file list: the last four

At the moment probably the easiest way for you to open the file is with the FILE menu.

At the very bottom you will see the names:

'1 Budget February.xls'

'2 Budget February on diskette ...'

'3 Budget.xls'

Under the FILE menu the last four workbooks you have edited are listed (so far you have only used three!).

When you select the BUDGET menu item, the corresponding workbook opens on your screen. This option works like a shortcut.

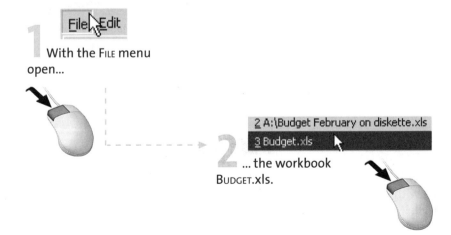

1 With the FILE menu open...

2 ... the workbook BUDGET.xls.

If you select the FILE menu item again, you will notice that the order of the recently used workbooks has changed.

1 Budget February.xls

2 A:\Budget February on diskette.xls

3 Budget.xls

The entry 'Budget' is now at the top, because it is the file which was last opened in Excel.

The recently used file list: the last nine

Under the TOOLS/OPTIONS menu item on the *General* tab you can increase the **number of recently used files** to a maximum of nine.

At the moment only the **last four** workbooks are displayed.

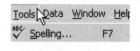

1 Select the TOOLS/OPTIONS menu command.

2 Choose the *General tab*.

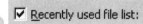 

3 Under *Recently used file list* increase the number with the mouse until the number '9' is displayed.

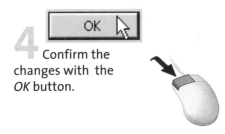

4 Confirm the changes with the *OK* button.

When you open the FILE menu, nothing much has changed. However, if you keep saving and opening workbooks one by one, the nine last files appear as entries.

Protecting data from unauthorised access

Ssshhh! Don't tell anyone! Top secret! You might find yourself in a situation where you want to keep your data secret from other people.

First, you must think of a password.

Passwords are **case-sensitive**.

Example:

The workbook 'Budget' is on your screen. You wish to protect it from unauthorised access, so that nobody but you can read it. Use the password 'Easy'.

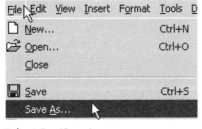

1 Select FILE/SAVE AS ...

Tools

~~Delete~~   Del
~~Rename~~
~~Print~~
Add to Favorites
Map Network Drive...
~~Properties~~

Web Options...
General Options...

Activate the *Tools* button, then
Options.

In the *Save Options* dialog box you can specify whether you want to prevent ...

1.) reading (*password to open*) or ...

2.) writing/modifying (*password to modify*).

3.) When you click on the *Write-protection recommendation* check box, you will receive a corresponding **recommendation** when opening the workbook.

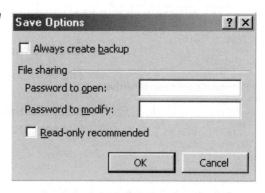

File sharing

Password to open: ****

Type the password 'Easy' in the *Password to open* box.

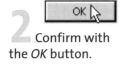

2 Confirm with the *OK* button.

3 **Type** the password **again**, spelling it exactly as before. Then confirm with the *OK* button.

4 **Save** the changes in the workbook with the relevant button.

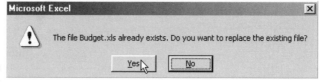

5 Confirm the substitution of the existing workbook (file) with *Yes*.

6 Close the workbook on your screen with the FILE/CLOSE menu option.

The workbook 'Budget' can from now on only be opened with the password 'Easy'.

The next time you open the workbook 'Budget', Excel prompts you to enter the **password**. Without it, you will not be able to open the workbook on your screen.

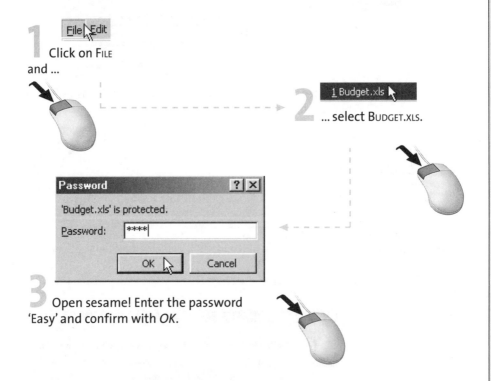

1 Click on FILE and ...

2 ... select BUDGET.XLS.

3 Open sesame! Enter the password 'Easy' and confirm with *OK*.

How to delete a password

Do you want to **remove** the read/write-protection from the workbook 'Budget'? Simply delete the password in the *Save options* dialog box with the Del key.

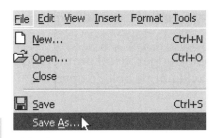

1 Select FILE/SAVE AS ...

2 Activate the *Tools* button, then select *Options*.

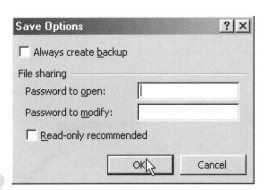

3 Press the Del key and confirm with *OK*.

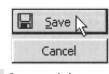

4 Save again!

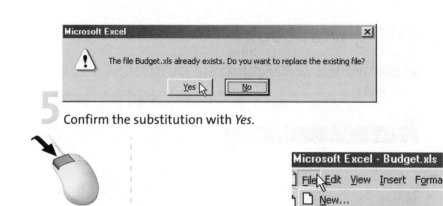

Confirm the substitution with *Yes*.

Close the workbook with FILE/CLOSE.

Now, when you open the workbook, you will no longer be asked for a password.

Select in the FILE
menu...

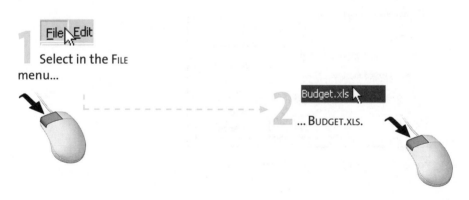

... BUDGET.XLS.

The workbook opens on your screen. Everything is back to normal.

Deleting workbooks

You wish to delete a workbook because you no longer need it. Well, throw it away!

Example:

The workbook 'Budget February' is to be deleted.

1 Open the WINDOW menu.

2 Choose the workbook 'Budget February.xls'.

A workbook which is to be deleted must not be opened on your screen.

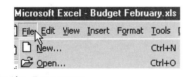

3 In the FILE menu ...

4 ... select CLOSE.

125

The choice is yours. You can either choose the *Save As* dialog box (FILE menu/ SAVE AS ...) or the OPEN dialog box (FILE menu /OPEN). In both dialog boxes you can delete an existing workbook/file.

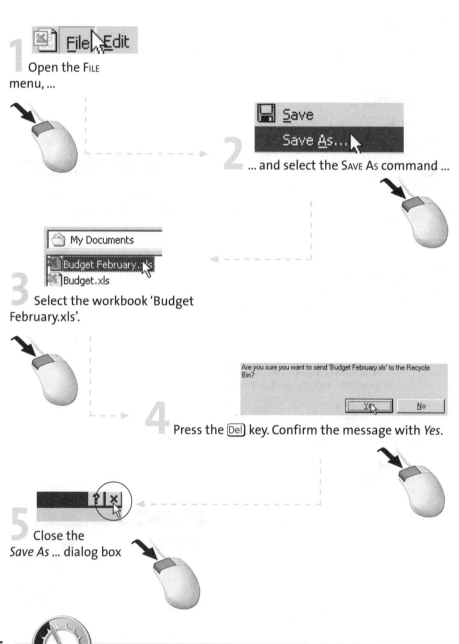

1 Open the FILE menu, ...

2 ... and select the SAVE AS command ...

3 Select the workbook 'Budget February.xls'.

Are you sure you want to send 'Budget February.xls' to the Recycle Bin?

Yes   No

4 Press the Del key. Confirm the message with *Yes*.

5 Close the *Save As* ... dialog box

The workbook has been deleted from your computer's hard drive!

Not completely though! On the Windows desktop there is a **Recycle Bin**. It not only allows you to delete files permanently, but also to restore accidentally deleted files.

Practise, practise and practise again!

Answer the following questions. The answers can be found in the Appendix.

Clicking on the button *Open* and the FILE/OPEN menu option lead ...

❏ to different dialog boxes

❏ to the *Open* dialog box

❏ to the *Save* dialog box

For read- and write-protection the password is ...

❏ important

❏ unimportant

A workbook can only be deleted, ...

❏ when it is open, i.e. is currently in use

❏ when it is not open, i.e. is currently not in use

Go through the following exercise. Execute the individual steps by yourself.

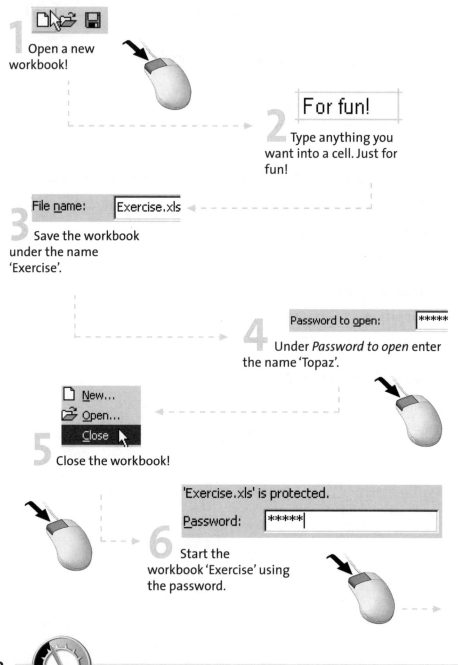

1 Open a new workbook!

2 Type anything you want into a cell. Just for fun!

For fun!

3 Save the workbook under the name 'Exercise'.

File name: | Exercise.xls

4 Under *Password to open* enter the name 'Topaz'.

Password to open: | *****

5 Close the workbook!

New...
Open...
Close

6 Start the workbook 'Exercise' using the password.

'Exercise.xls' is protected.
Password: | *****|

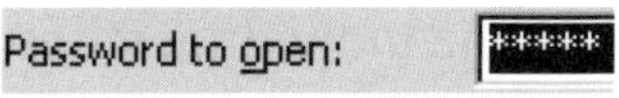

7 Delete the password.

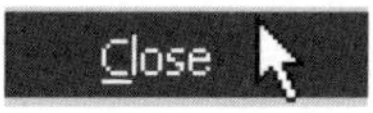

8 Close the file 'Exercise'!

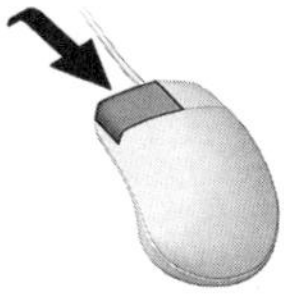

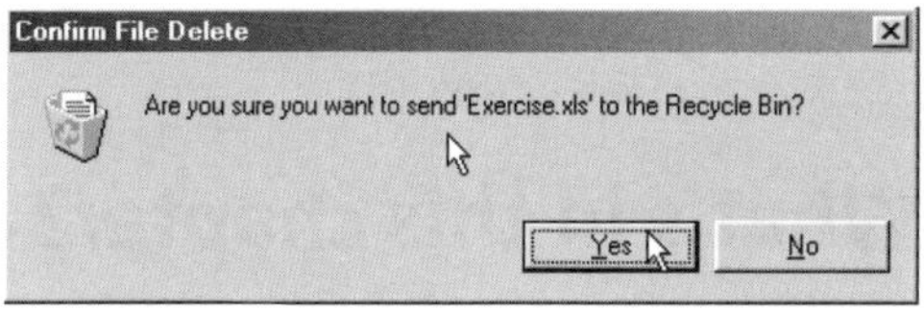

9 Delete the workbook.

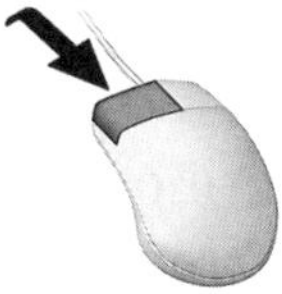

CAUTION

If you are going to switch off your PC, do not forget to remove the diskette, which you have used in this chapter.

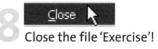

What's in this chapter?

Entering the same data over and over again is extremely tedious and totally unnecessary. That is why in Excel 2000 you can quickly copy and fill in cell contents. With a few practical examples you will soon master the functions of the program.

With the help of the mouse pointer you can not only avoid having to repeat entries but you can also make creating lists a much easier task.

You already know about:

You are going to learn about:

Copying cells

You do not have to keep entering identical cell contents.
There are several alternative options in Excel. One can be
found on the Standard toolbar: first, you click on the *Copy* button and
then the *Paste* button.

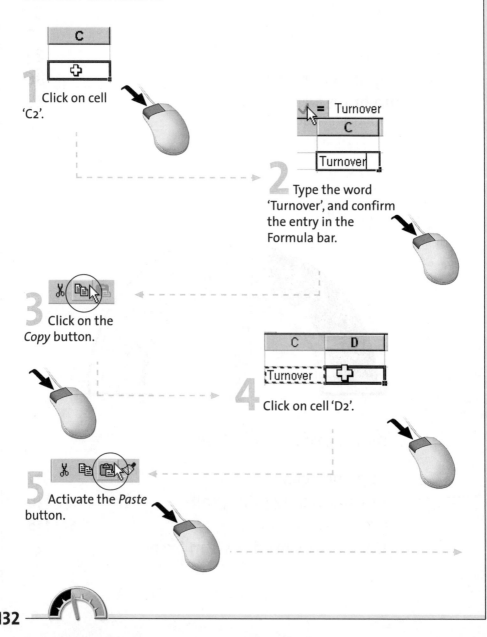

Click on cell
'C2'.

Type the word
'Turnover', and confirm
the entry in the
Formula bar.

Click on the
Copy button.

Click on cell 'D2'.

Activate the *Paste*
button.

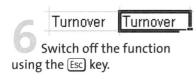

6 Switch off the function using the (Esc) key.

The contents of cell 'C2' are now copied to cell 'D2'.

Copying with the mouse pointer

You can do this even faster by using the **mouse pointer**. You must position it exactly on the **fill handle** (the small black box).

It turns into a small black plus (+).

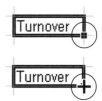

In the Appendix **(The mouse pointer and its appearance)** you can find detailed information about the functions of the mouse pointer.

1 Position the mouse pointer exactly on the **fill handle**. (It should turn into a '+'.)

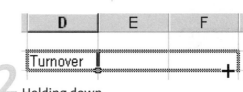

2 Holding down the mouse button, drag it two cells to the right, to cell 'F2'.

Turnover	Turnover	Turnover	Turnover

3 Release the left mouse button!

Turnover	Turnover	Turnover	Turnover

4 Remove the marking with a mouse-click anywhere on the worksheet.

With the mouse pointer you can also copy cells that are **not next to each other**.

Only when the **mouse pointer** has the shape of a *white cross*, it is possible to mark several cells.

If you want to copy **several cells** at once, you first have to **mark** them so that Excel knows which cell contents have to be duplicated.

C
Turnover

1 Click on cell 'C2'.

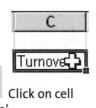

Turnover	Turnover	Turnover	Turnover

2 Holding down the mouse button, mark up to cell 'F2'. Release the mouse button.

This time you copy cell contents into cells that are not next to each other. You have to press the Ctrl key, as well as the mouse button. A small plus (+) appears at the mouse pointer. The copy function is activated.

1
Turnover | Turnover | Turnover | Turnover

Position the mouse pointer on the edge of the marking. It turns into a *white arrow*.

Turnover

2 Press the Ctrl key ...

Turnover | Turnover | Turnover | Turnover

C9:F9

3 ... and holding down the mouse button drag the cells downwards, until **ScreenTips** (the yellow box) displays the cell range 'C9:F9'.

135

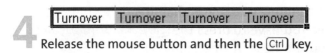

4 Release the mouse button and then the (Ctrl) key.

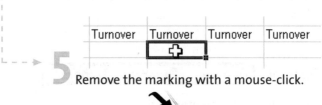

5 Remove the marking with a mouse-click.

Automatically filling cells

To avoid those never-ending boring repetitions, Excel offers a quicker entry option.

If you want to enter the **names of months**, you do not need to bother entering each

Jan	Feb	Mar	Apr
January	February	March	April

one. Excel recognises abbreviations such as 'Jan, Feb, Mar' and so on.

1 Click on cell 'B4'.

2 Enter the month 'January'.

You can write the whole word 'January', or choose the abbreviation 'Jan'.

When you position the mouse pointer on the fill handle and, holding down the mouse button, drag into other cells, Excel automatically fills these with the following months.

For example, if you start with 'April' and fill the cells to the right, Excel continues with 'May, June, July, ...'.

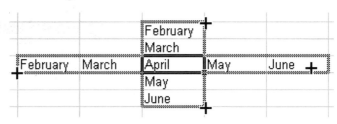

However, if you drag to the left, the list runs: 'March, February, January, December, ... '. This also works for the cells above and below.

You can also use the AutoFill function for **names of days**.

Mon	Tue	Wed	Thu
Monday	Tuesday	Wednesday	Thursday

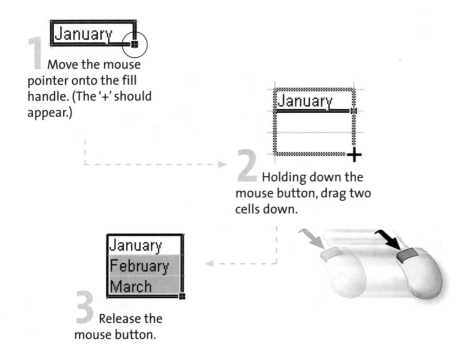

1 Move the mouse pointer onto the fill handle. (The '+' should appear.)

2 Holding down the mouse button, drag two cells down.

3 Release the mouse button.

Which lists are there?

An overview of the lists can be found on the *Custom Lists* tab under the TOOLS/OPTIONS menu option.

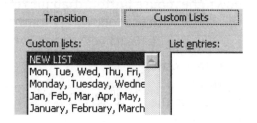

Creating custom lists

The lists for months and days are already set up in Excel. However, you can modify or add custom lists. You can even define a different order.

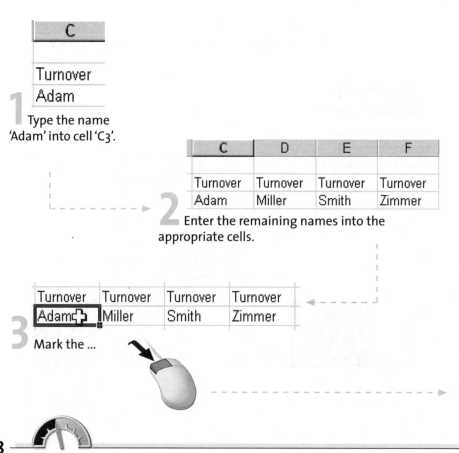

1 Type the name 'Adam' into cell 'C3'.

2 Enter the remaining names into the appropriate cells.

3 Mark the ...

4 ... cells with the names.

Open the TOOLS menu, ...

6 ... and choose OPTIONS.

| Transition | Custom Lists | Chart |

7 Choose the *Custom Lists* tab.

8 Click on the *Import* button.

Further options for creating your own lists can be found in the exercises at the end of this chapter.

The new entries appear in the list.

With the *Delete* button you can remove the list again.

139

Have you followed the instructions faithfully? Has Excel accepted your list? In the next step you will find out, by simply testing it!

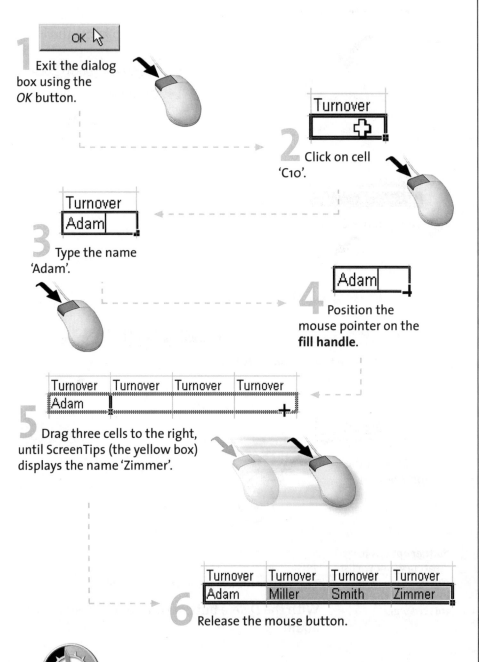

1 Exit the dialog box using the *OK* button.

2 Click on cell 'C10'.

3 Type the name 'Adam'.

4 Position the mouse pointer on the **fill handle**.

5 Drag three cells to the right, until ScreenTips (the yellow box) displays the name 'Zimmer'.

6 Release the mouse button.

1, 2, 3 ... Automatic lists in Excel

You must also press the Ctrl key; otherwise the value is only copied.

Numbers for incremental lists do not need to be typed in each time. Also, you do not have to start with '1'. Excel only needs to know the opening value.

1 Click on cell 'A4'.

2 Enter the number '1'.

3 Move the mouse pointer onto the **fill handle**.

4 Press the Ctrl key.

After you have dragged the mouse and the result – here '1,2,3' – is displayed, you must be careful to release the mouse button first and then the Ctrl key, otherwise the operation will not work.

5 Drag two cells down.

6 First release the mouse button and then the Ctrl key.

Excel offers you further list options. You can use the AutoFill function not only for numeric values, but also for entries such as:

➔ Vehicle 1, Vehicle 2, Vehicle 3 ...

➔ Area 1, Area 2, Area 3 ...

➔ Shop Assistant 1, Shop Assistant 2, Shop Assistant 3 ...

➔ Constituency 1, Constituency 2, Constituency 3 ...

CAUTION

AutoFill only works if you enter first the text and then the number. You do not need to press the Ctrl key!

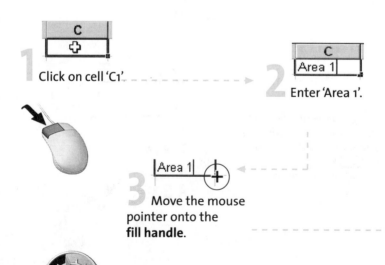

1 Click on cell 'C1'.

2 Enter 'Area 1'.

3 Move the mouse pointer onto the **fill handle**.

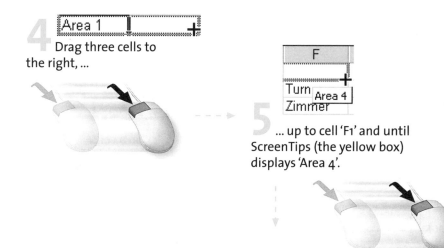

4 Drag three cells to the right, ...

5 ... up to cell 'F1' and until ScreenTips (the yellow box) displays 'Area 4'.

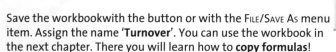

6 Release the mouse button.

Save the workbookwith the button or with the FILE/SAVE As menu item. Assign the name '**Turnover**'. You can use the workbook in the next chapter. There you will learn how to **copy formulas**!

Practise, practise and practise again!

In the following exercises, you will get to know further options for copying with the **fill function**.

I. Exercise

Example:

You wish Excel to display all leap years (every four years) from the year 1960 up to the year 2000.

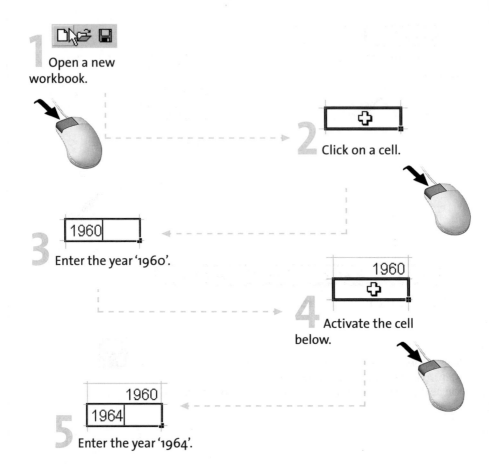

1 Open a new workbook.

2 Click on a cell.

3 Enter the year '1960'.

4 Activate the cell below.

5 Enter the year '1964'.

To create a separate list, you will need to tell Excel what you want to list. In this case, a list with a four year gap between the individual items is to be created.

First you need to **mark** both cells.

You do **not** need to press the Ctrl key.

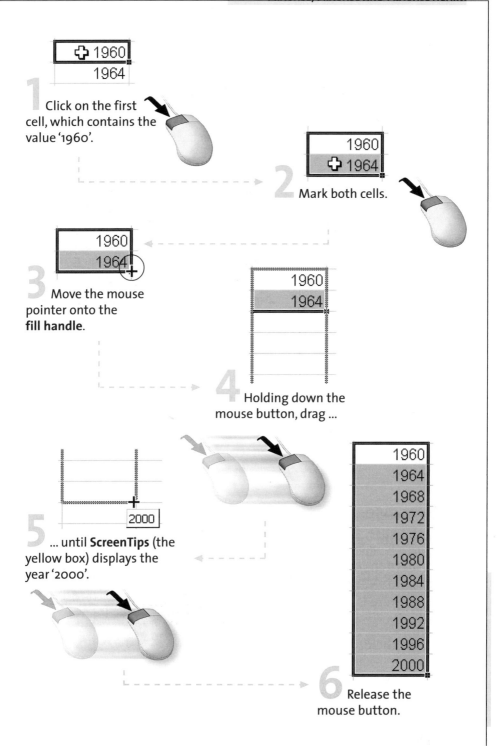

1 Click on the first cell, which contains the value '1960'.

2 Mark both cells.

3 Move the mouse pointer onto the **fill handle**.

4 Holding down the mouse button, drag ...

5 ... until **ScreenTips** (the yellow box) displays the year '2000'.

6 Release the mouse button.

II. Exercise

Mon	Area 1	1	Serial No.1
		3	

1 Enter the following values on your worksheet.

Mon	Area 1	1	Serial No.1
Tue	Area 2	3	Serial No.2
Wed	Area 3	5	Serial No.3
Thu	Area 4	7	Serial No.4
Fri	Area 5	9	Serial No.5
Sat	Area 6	11	Serial No.6
Sun	Area 7	13	Serial No.7

2 Draw up the lists with the help of AutoFill.

III. Exercise

How to create your own lists

In this chapter, you have learnt how to create your own lists. However, there is an alternative method!

Again, use the *Custom Lists* tab.

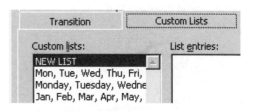

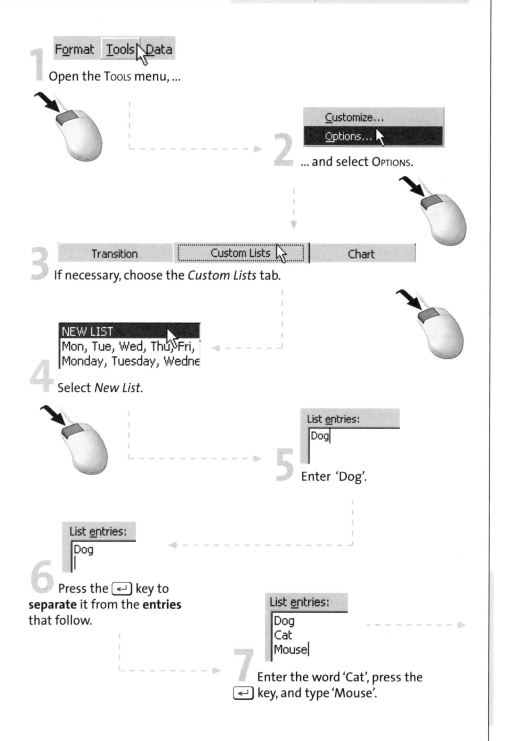

1 Open the Tools menu, ...

2 ... and select Options.

3 If necessary, choose the *Custom Lists* tab.

4 Select *New List*.

5 Enter 'Dog'.

6 Press the ⏎ key to **separate** it from the **entries** that follow.

7 Enter the word 'Cat', press the ⏎ key, and type 'Mouse'.

147

8 Confirm the new list
with the *Add* button.

9 Exit the dialog box
with *OK*.

The new list on your worksheet.

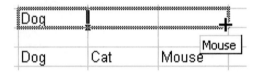

IV. Exercise

Deleting lists?

When lists become unnecessary, you can delete them.

1 Select the Tools/Options menu option again.
If necessary choose the *Custom Lists* tab.

Click on the list you want to delete 'Dog, Cat, Mouse'.

Remove the list with the *Delete* button.

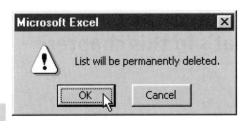

Confirm with *OK*. The entry 'Dog, Cat, Mouse' has been deleted.

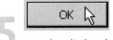

Exit the dialog box.

149

What's in this chapter?

When you create a new calculation in Excel 2000, you enter the appropriate formula every single time, to get the right result. Why complicate things for yourself? Things could be so much easier! Simply copy the same formula for several calculations.

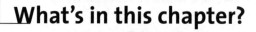

	Turnover Adam	Turnover Miller	Turnover Smith	Turnover Zimmer
April	10000	40000	15000	20000
May	20000	10000	5000	5000
June	30000	20000	2500	2000

You already know about:

You are going to learn about:

Copying formulas

Use the workbook 'Turnover' from Chapter 7.

1 Open the FILE menu, ...

2 ... and select the workbook 'Turnover'.

> If you have skipped the chapter, just enter the data now.

You do not need to use the following numbers. The aim of this example is to illustrate the function 'copy formulas '.

	Adam	Miller	Smith	Zimmer
January	10000	25000	10000	5000
February	25000	30000	20000	10000
March	3000	40000	10000	5000

1 Enter these numbers into the cells:

'C4':   10000
'C5':   25000
'C6':   30000
'D4':   25000
'D5':   30000
'D6':   40000
'E4':   10000
'E5':   20000
'E6':   10000
'F4':   5000
'F5':   10000
'F6':   5000

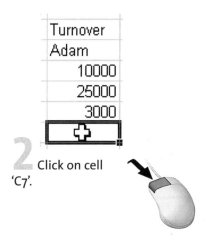

Turnover
Adam
10000
25000
3000

2 Click on cell 'C7'.

Next, calculate the sum of the first column 'Adam'.

1 Activate the *AutoSum* button.

2 Confirm the formula with the Formula bar.

Calculation has been carried out. However, Excel can do more: copying formulas .

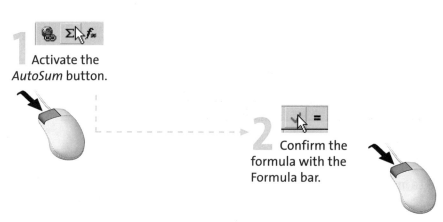

Adam	Miller	Smith	Zimmer
10000	25000	10000	5000
25000	30000	20000	10000
3000	40000	10000	5000
65000	95000	40000	20000

Move the mouse pointer onto the **fill handle**.

Holding down the left mouse button, **copy** the formulas into the remaining cells.

153

The program knows that all the cells up to the text need to be included in the calculation.

1
65000

Place the mouse pointer on the **fill handle**.

10000	25000	10000	5000
25000	30000	20000	10000
30000	40000	10000	5000
65000			

2 Holding down the mouse button, drag up to cell 'F7'

10000	25000	10000	5000
25000	30000	20000	10000
30000	40000	10000	5000
65000	95000	40000	20000

3 Release the mouse button.

The same is also possible for vertical calculations.

50000

January	10000	25000	10000	5000
February	25000	30000	20000	10000
March	30000	40000	10000	5000

In this example, you are calculating the turnover for the months of January, February and March. First calculate the sum for January.

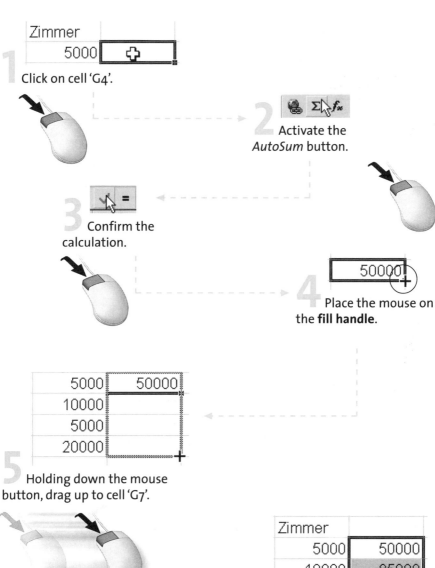

Click on cell 'G4'.

Activate the *AutoSum* button.

Confirm the calculation.

Place the mouse on the **fill handle**.

Holding down the mouse button, drag up to cell 'G7'.

Release the mouse button.

155

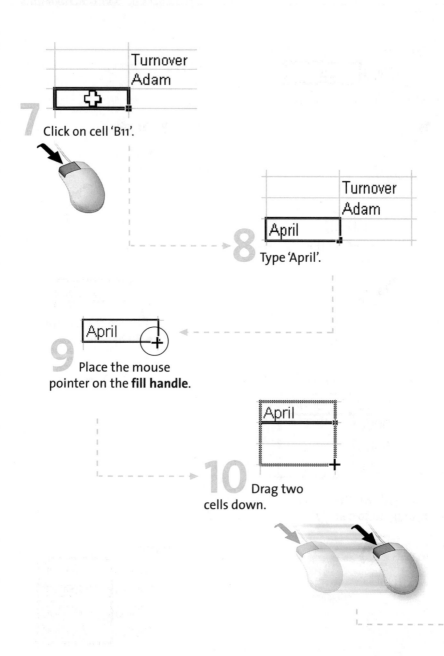

Turnover
Adam

7 Click on cell 'B11'.

Turnover
Adam

April

8 Type 'April'.

April

9 Place the mouse pointer on the **fill handle**.

April

10 Drag two cells down.

	Adam	Miller	Smith	Zimmer
April	10000	40000	15000	20000
May	20000	10000	5000	5000
June	30000	20000	2500	2000

11 Type the following numbers into the corresponding cells:

'C11': 10000
'C12': 20000
'C13': 30000
'D11': 40000
'D12': 10000
'D13': 20000
'E11': 15000
'E12': 5000
'E13': 2500
'F11': 20000
'F12': 5000
'F13': 2000

Copying formulas into other cell ranges

You can also copy formulas into cells that are not next to each other. You can use for example the *Copy* button and then the *Paste* button. (With the (Esc) button you switch off the function again.)

However, you can also use the mouse: **mark** the formulas and then drag them into the appropriate cell range.

Adam
10000
25000
30000
⬧65000

1 Click on cell 'C7'.

10000	25000	10000	5000
25000	30000	20000	10000
30000	40000	10000	5000
65000	95000	40000 ⊕	20000

2 Mark up to (and including) cell 'F7'.

Move the mouse pointer onto the outline of the marking. It changes into an arrow. Holding down the mouse button, drag the contents into the new cells.

You also need to press the Ctrl key.

40000

1 Place the mouse pointer onto the outline of the marking and hold down the Ctrl key.

	Turnover	Turnover	Turnover	Turnover
	Adam	Miller	Smith	Zimmer
April	10000	40000	15000	20000
May	20000	10000	5000	5000
June	30000	20000	2500	2000

2 Holding down the mouse button, drag the cell contents into the cell range 'C14 to F14'.

After you have dragged with
the mouse, you **first** have to
release the mouse button and
then the (Ctrl) key, otherwise
Excel will not copy the formula,
but will only move it.

Turnover	Turnover	Turnover	Turnover
Adam	Miller	Smith	Zimmer
10000	40000	15000	20000
20000	10000	5000	5000
30000	20000	2500	2000
60000	70000	22500	27000

First release the mouse button and **then** the
(Ctrl) key.

159

What's in this chapter?

Currencies ahoy – exchange rate
calculations! Do you like travelling?
Wouldn't it be nice to know how many
pounds you get to a dollar, franc, 100 yen
or 1000 lire? When you
have created the next
workbook, you will
always know how
much you get for
ten, 20, 30, or 50
pounds.

You do not have
to recalculate
everything every
time the
exchange rate
fluctuates.
You can also convert euros
into pounds.

You already know about:

You are going to learn about:

Entering currencies

The next workbook will calculate how many US dollars you get for your money. You will obviously remember that you cannot calculate with **text**.

When you enter '$1' for one dollar on the keyboard, the cell contents align **left**. This means that Excel does not count the entry as a number to calculate with, but 'only' as **text**.

$1

CAUTION

Cells that contain currency values must be formatted in currency style.

The cell has to be 'switched' – **formatted** – to dollars. When you click on the *Currency* button, the abbreviation '£' for pound sterling is inserted. However, what about other currencies? To display other currencies, call up the FORMAT/CELLS menu command.

TIP

Instead of choosing the fairly long-winded method with the FORMAT/CELLS menu option to open the *Format Cells* dialog box, you can use the much quicker keyboard shortcut [Ctrl] + [1]. First press the [Ctrl] key, hold it down, then type '1'. Then release both buttons.

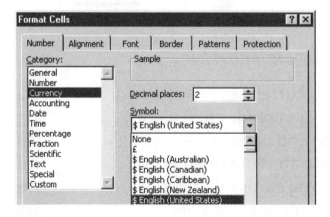

As you are working with numbers, activate the *Number* tab. Under *Category*, a list is displayed. In this exercise you will calculate with **currency values**, thus you need the *Currency item*.

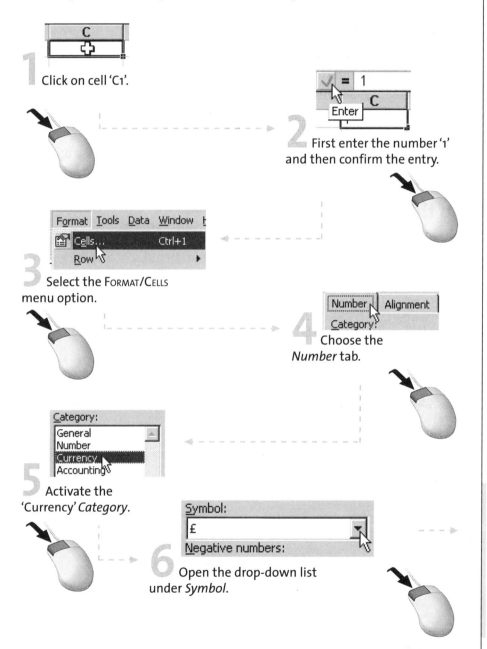

1 Click on cell 'C1'.

2 First enter the number '1' and then confirm the entry.

3 Select the FORMAT/CELLS menu option.

4 Choose the *Number* tab.

5 Activate the 'Currency' *Category*.

6 Open the drop-down list under *Symbol*.

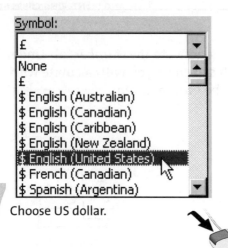

7 Choose US dollar.

To the point

On the *Number* tab you can also specify the number of **decimal places**. As you do not use any for your calculation of dollars, change it to 'o'.

The **Preview window** is a great help. Here you can see what your value will look like when you confirm the format with *OK*.

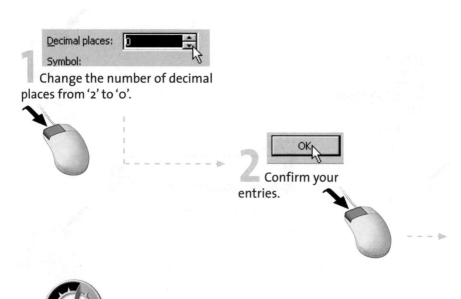

1 Change the number of decimal places from '2' to 'o'.

2 Confirm your entries.

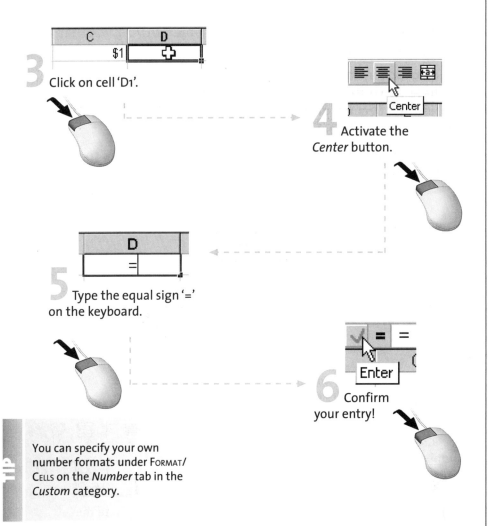

3 Click on cell 'D1'.

4 Activate the *Center* button.

Center

5 Type the equal sign '=' on the keyboard.

6 Confirm your entry!

Enter

TIP

You can specify your own number formats under FORMAT/ CELLS on the *Number* tab in the *Custom* category.

Entering pence (decimal places)

To display a number in '£' format, you will use the *Currency* button. By default, the entry has **two decimal places** (£ 0.63).

However, you know from the news that on the foreign-exchange market the dollar is fixed with **three** decimal places (£ 0.632). You can choose the longer way using the FORMAT menu /CELLS/ *Number* tab and specify '3' under *Decimal Places*.

It is quicker and easier with the buttons. You have two buttons to choose from. With one you add decimal places and with the other you remove them.

+.0 .00	0.632	Increase Decimal
.00 +.0	0.63	Decrease Decimal

As there are already two decimal places (£ 0.63), you need to add another one (£ 0.632).

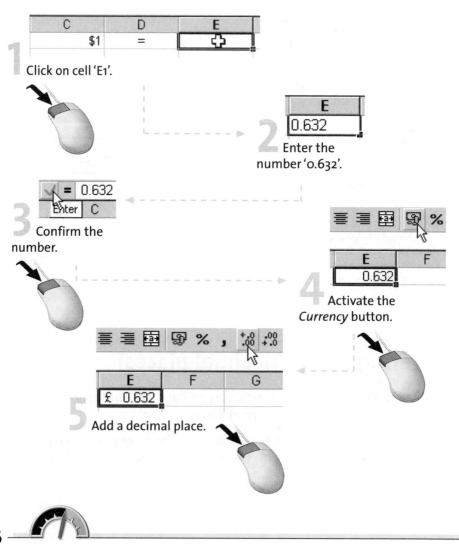

1 Click on cell 'E1'.

C	D	E
$1	=	✚

2 Enter the number '0.632'.

E
0.632

3 Confirm the number.

✓	=	0.632
Enter	C	

4 Activate the *Currency* button.

E	F
0.632	

5 Add a decimal place.

E	F	G
£ 0.632		

Applying formats

First enter the dollar values. To specify the dollar format, we do not choose the longer method with the menu, but the *Format Painter* button. With this button, you can **apply** the **currency format** and thus save time. The '$' symbol already exists in one of the cells. You need to activate the cell. One click on the *Format Painter* button, and you can 'paint over' the cells where you want to display the dollar format, too.

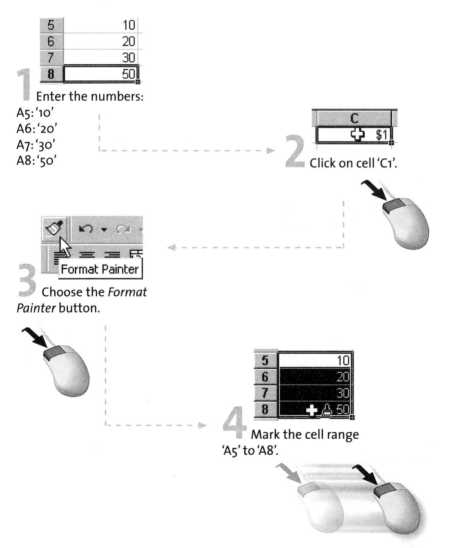

1 Enter the numbers:
A5: '10'
A6: '20'
A7: '30'
A8: '50'

2 Click on cell 'C1'.

3 Choose the *Format Painter* button.

4 Mark the cell range 'A5' to 'A8'.

Copying and Pasting

You need the equal sign '=' a total of four times. It could be worse!
You can enter the signs one after the other. But why bother, when you can do it in a much easier way!
You can **copy** the cell that already contains the centred equal sign. Then you use the **fill handle**, and all cells will contain the (centred) equal sign.

$10	=
$20	=
$30	=
$50	=

First option:

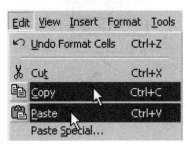

You can copy with the menu. However, this is the longest way. Click on the cell you wish to copy from, call up the EDIT/ COPY menu command . Then click on the cell you wish to copy to, and execute the EDIT/INSERT menu command.
(A total of six mouse operations!)

Second option:

A shorter way is with the buttons. Click on the cell you want to copy from, activate the *Copy* button and insert the contents into the cell you are copying to with the *Paste* button. (A total of four mouse operations!)

Third option:

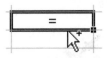

The **drag and drop method** is surely the quickest way of copying. Copying cell contents with the drag and drop method is the same as cutting.
In addition, you need to press the Ctrl key.

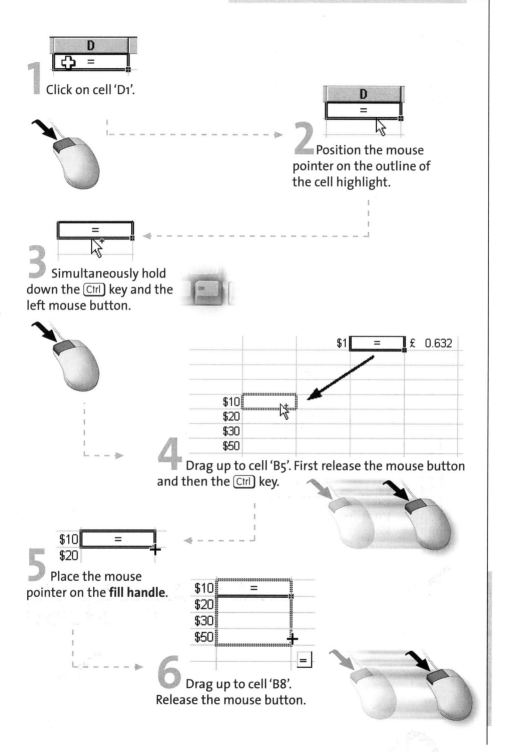

1 Click on cell 'D1'.

2 Position the mouse pointer on the outline of the cell highlight.

3 Simultaneously hold down the Ctrl key and the left mouse button.

4 Drag up to cell 'B5'. First release the mouse button and then the Ctrl key.

5 Place the mouse pointer on the **fill handle**.

6 Drag up to cell 'B8'. Release the mouse button.

169

Absolute references

Now you only need the FORMULA for the calculation. If one dollar is equal to £ 0.632, then £ 10, £ 20, £ 30, or £ 50 are equal to 10, 20, 30 or 50 times the amount respectively.

 1 dollar = £ 0.632

10 dollars = £ 0.632 * 10

20 dollars = £ 0.632 * 20

30 dollars = £ 0.632 * 30

50 dollars = £ 0.632 * 50

Since in Excel you do not only calculate with numbers but also with cells, the formulas are:

A5 = E1 * A5

A6 = E1 * A6

A7 = E1 * A7

A8 = E1 * A8

	A	B	C	D	E
1			$1	=	£ 0.632
2					
3					
4					
5	$10	=			
6	$20	=			
7	$30	=			
8	$50	=			

1 Click on cell 'C5'.

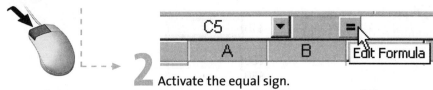

C5 ▼ =

A	B	
		Edit Formula

2 Activate the equal sign.

Moving the Formula bar

Now you are probably faced with the problem that the Formula bar is covering the cells 'C1' to 'E1', with which you want to work.

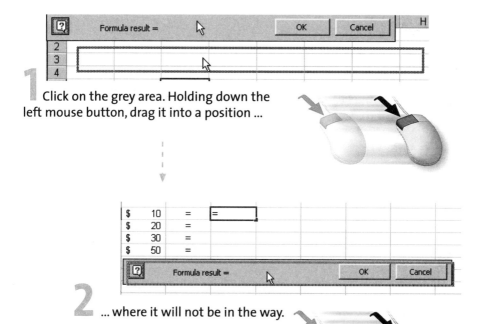

1 Click on the grey area. Holding down the left mouse button, drag it into a position ...

2 ... where it will not be in the way.

Copying formulas

Let's continue with the worksheet. Enter the formula outlined above. For the first row it runs as follows:

A5 = E1 * A5

As the **formula** is **identical** for all cells (= relative references) you can use the **fill handle** to copy it into the cells below.

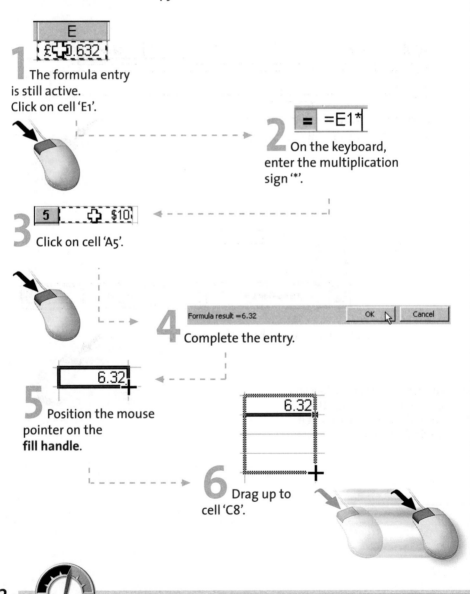

1 The formula entry is still active.
Click on cell 'E1'.

2 On the keyboard, enter the multiplication sign '*'.

3 Click on cell 'A5'.

4 Complete the entry.

Formula result =6.32   OK   Cancel

5 Position the mouse pointer on the **fill handle**.

6 Drag up to cell 'C8'.

No values or wrong values?

What is happening? In three cells there is no value or there is only 'o'. That cannot be correct! Only the value in the first cell is correct. Why?

$10	=	6.32
$20	=	0
$30	=	0
$50	=	0

When copying formulas, Excel always counts 'one up'.

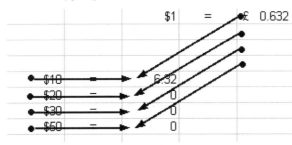

Thus, the following cells **refer** to the wrong data.

Cell references

The value for one dollar is always in one and the **same cell** (here: 'E1'). Each copied formula refers to it. 'Counting on' is thus wrong here. The program has to be instructed to get the value only from **one particular cell**.

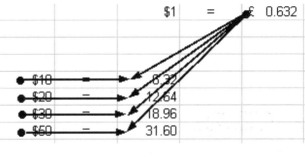

This is done with the help of the **dollar sign**, which in this context is not connected to the currency. '$E$1' means that the looked for value is always in cell E1. Now Excel no longer carries out calculations when copying formulas.

If several formulas refer to only one cell when copying, this must be specified with the dollar sign $$. Do not get it confused with the dollar currency!

The dollar signs can be entered before or after the entry. If you have already entered the cell name, you only need to press the F4 key.

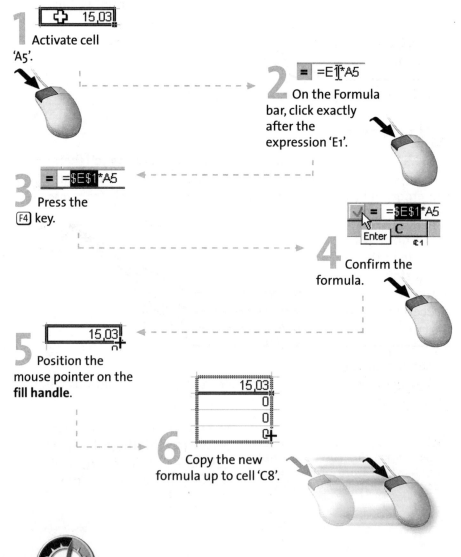

1 Activate cell 'A5'.

2 On the Formula bar, click exactly after the expression 'E1'.

3 Press the `F4` key.

4 Confirm the formula.

5 Position the mouse pointer on the fill handle.

6 Copy the new formula up to cell 'C8'.

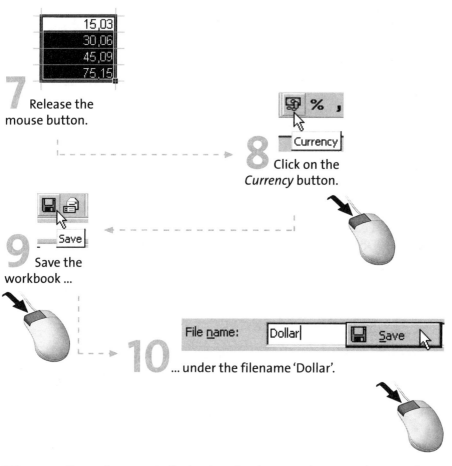

7 Release the
mouse button.

8 Click on the
Currency button.

9 Save the
workbook ...

10 ... under the filename 'Dollar'.

Whenever the exchange rate fluctuates, simply enter the new value into the
cell.

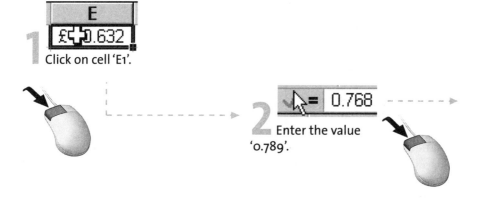

1 Click on cell 'E1'.

2 Enter the value
'0.789'.

175

$10	=	£	7.68
$20	=	£	15.36
$30	=	£	23.04
$50	=	£	38.40

3 The values adjust according to the new exchange rate.

Converting euros into pounds

Now the euro has been introduced as a new currency. With the help of Excel you can create your own euro converter. Use the existing workbook 'Dollar', which is still on your screen. You only have to swap 'Dollar' for 'Euro'.

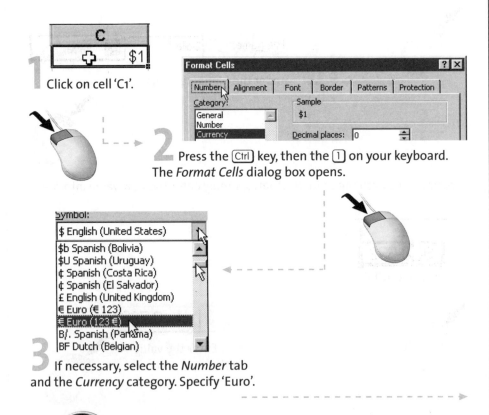

1 Click on cell 'C1'.

2 Press the Ctrl key, then the 1 on your keyboard. The *Format Cells* dialog box opens.

3 If necessary, select the *Number* tab and the *Currency* category. Specify 'Euro'.

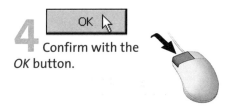

4 Confirm with the *OK* button.

Cell 'C1' has been formatted with the euro symbol. Now you only need to transfer the format to the remaining cells.

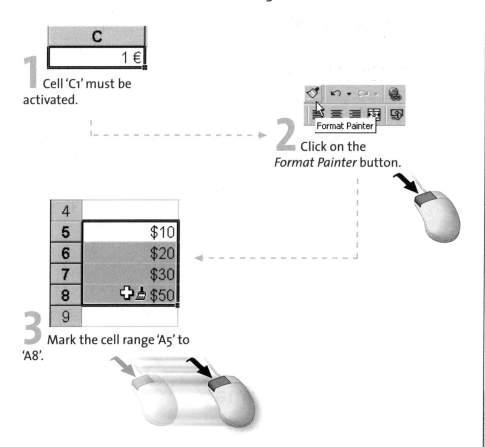

1 Cell 'C1' must be activated.

2 Click on the *Format Painter* button.

3 Mark the cell range 'A5' to 'A8'.

Now enter the exchange rate for the euro (£ 1 = 0.6478 euros). As soon as you have done this, you will know how many euros you get for your pounds.

177

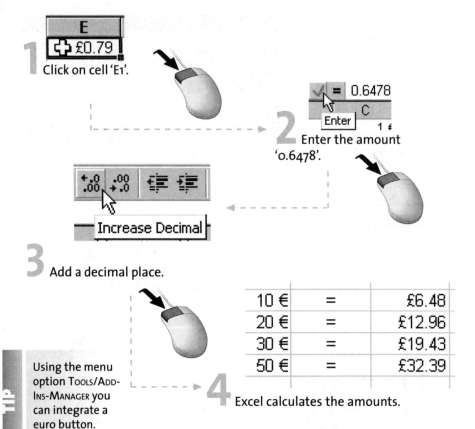

1 Click on cell 'E1'.

2 Enter the amount '0.6478'.

3 Add a decimal place.

10 €	=	£6.48
20 €	=	£12.96
30 €	=	£19.43
50 €	=	£32.39

4 Excel calculates the amounts.

Save the workbook with the FILE/SAVE AS menu command. Assign the name 'Euro'.

Deleting number formats

You need the *Format Cells* dialog box and the *Number* tab. Under *Category* select either *Standard* or *Number*. Then activate a 'normal' number format. As soon as you confirm your entries with the *OK* button or the ⏎ key, the new format is applied to the numbers.

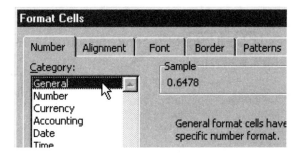

CAUTION

Number formats can only be removed with the *Format Cells* dialog box on the *Number* tab.

An overview of number formats:

Format	Name	Number
0	Whole number	7
0.00	Two fixed decimals	7.77
#,##0	Whole number with thousand separator	7,777
- #,##0	Negative, whole number with thousand separator	-7,777
#,##0.00	Whole number with thousand separator and two decimals	7,777.77

Date formats

You can insert the current date in Excel. You do not need to start the Function Wizard. The formula is relatively EASY, so that you can write it yourself. Enter the **equal sign**, so that Excel knows that a formula is going to follow.

What is the date today?

If you want to get the time and date, enter '**NOW()**'.

```
= | =NOW()
       C
   22/07/99 13:12
```

With the entry '**TODAY()**' you get the current date.

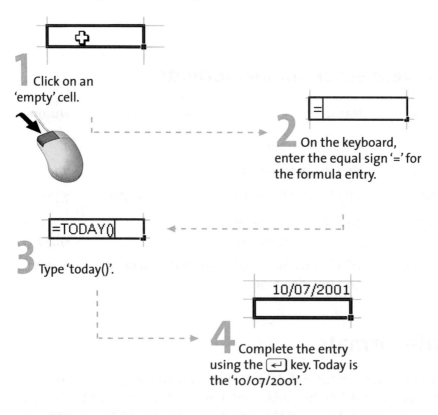

1 Click on an 'empty' cell.

2 On the keyboard, enter the equal sign '=' for the formula entry.

```
=TODAY()
```

3 Type 'today()'.

```
10/07/2001
```

4 Complete the entry using the ⏎ key. Today is the '10/07/2001'.

However, Excel offers even more. If you, for example want to specify on an invoice that it must be paid in 30 days, enter '=today()+30'.

Formula	Result
=now()	Current date and time
=today()+7	Next week
=today()+30	Current date plus 30 days
=today()-7	Last week
=today()-30	Current date minus 30 days

The times they are a-changin'

Your computer should always have the current date and time. As a user of Windows 95, 98, or Windows NT you are always informed about what time it is. You can see it on the **Task bar** at the bottom of your screen. Of course, there is no guarantee that the displayed time or date are correct, unless your computer is connected to an atomic clock. Position the mouse pointer on the **Clock display** and double-click on it. In the *Date and time* tab you can set the correct time and date.

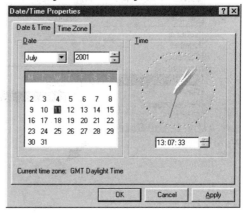

Windows 95 and 98 automatically adjust the clock for the **Summer/Winter** time switch.

Formatted dates

The default format of the date is: '10.07.01'. You can also display it differently. For example, change it to ' July 10, 2001'. You can also display the date differently. You only need to change the **format**.

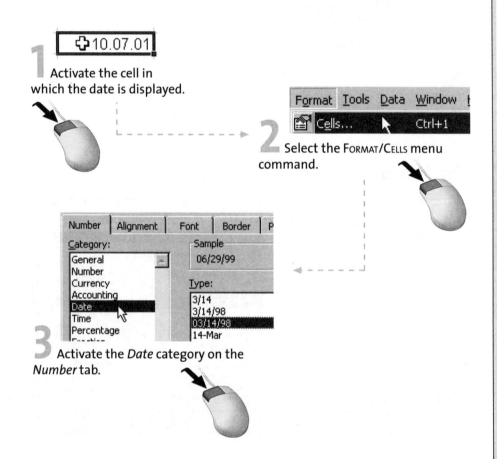

1 Activate the cell in which the date is displayed.

2 Select the FORMAT/CELLS menu command.

3 Activate the *Date* category on the *Number* tab.

Under *Type* you can see the various available formats. When you click on one, you can preview it in the window. Do not be confused by the displayed date – here 'April 14, 1998'. It is not an April fool's joke. What matters here is the format of the date.

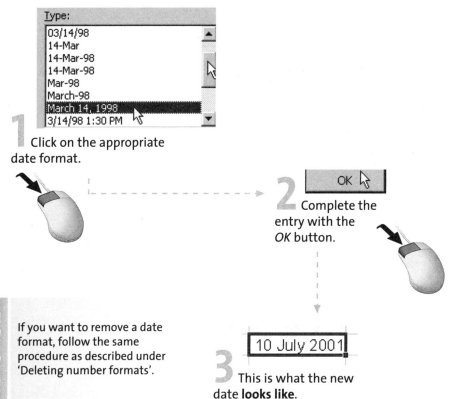

Type:
03/14/98
14-Mar
14-Mar-98
14-Mar-98
Mar-98
March-98
March 14, 1998
3/14/98 1:30 PM

Click on the appropriate date format.

OK

Complete the entry with the *OK* button.

If you want to remove a date format, follow the same procedure as described under 'Deleting number formats'.

10 July 2001

This is what the new date **looks like**.

Practise, practise and practise again!

Now you have to work on your own. Solve the exercises independently and think carefully about the formulas.

To assist you, the answers and formulas are displayed immediately after the task. Remember to cover the answers!

Exercise 1:

	B	C	D
1	**Omission Fee**		
2			
3	Omission Charge	£20.00	
4	Processing Fee	£5.00	
5			
6			
7	Net Amount	Amount Payable	
8			
9	£725.00		
10	£800.00		
11	£900.00		
12	£1,000.00		
13	£2,500.00		
14	£10,000.00		

Answer:

	B	C	D		Amount Payable
1	**Omission Fee**				
2					
3	Omission Charge	£20.00			
4	Processing Fee	£5.00			
5					
6					
7	Net Amount	Amount Payable			
8					
9	£725.00	£750.00			=$C$3+$C$4+B9
10	£800.00	£825.00			=$C$3+$C$4+B10
11	£900.00	£925.00			=$C$3+$C$4+B11
12	£1,000.00	£1,025.00			=$C$3+$C$4+B12
13	£2,500.00	£2,525.00			=$C$3+$C$4+B13
14	£10,000.00	£10,025.00			=$C$3+$C$4+B14
15					

Change the omission charge: £ 10, £ 15, £ 30

Change the processing fee: £ 10, £ 15, £ 20

Exercise 2:

	A	B	C	D
1		Kitty Bank		
2				
3		Interest for your savings		
4				
5		Interest =	0.03	
6				
7	Amount saved	Interest	Amount paid	
8	£1,000.00			
9	£2,000.00			
10	£3,000.00			
11	£5,000.00			
12	£10,000.00			

Answer:

	A	B	C	D
1		Kitty Bank		
2				
3		Interest for your savings		
4				
5		Interest =	0.03	
6				
7	Amount saved	Interest	Amount paid	
8	£1,000.00	£30.00	£1,030.00	
9	£2,000.00	£60.00	£2,060.00	
10	£3,000.00	£90.00	£3,090.00	
11	£5,000.00	£150.00	£5,150.00	
12	£10,000.00	£300.00	£10,300.00	

Interest	Amount paid
=$C$5*A8	£1,030.00
=$C$5*A9	£2,060.00
=$C$5*A10	£3,090.00
=$C$5*A11	£5,150.00
=$C$5*A12	£10,300.00

Change the interest rate: 0.02, 0.025, 0.01

What's in this chapter?

In business, in elections, on food packaging, or when buying alcoholic drinks, percentage values are all important. In a distribution, the percentage figures make it easier for you to recognise the size of the shares. Which is the higher value? 1,800 euros out of your pocket money of 4,500 euros, or 3,120 euros out of 7,800 euros? Sure, you can buy more in your local corner shop with 3,120 euro, but in per cent the amounts are equal (40 %)! How do you find out the per cent values? Excel offers a quick and easy option.

Amounts	Percent
£1,000.00	12%
£ 500.00	6%
£ 300.00	3%
£2,300.00	27%
£4,500.00	52%

Naming cells

In this chapter, you will carry out a simple operation without any 'frills'. You are going to list numbers, add them up, and convert the individual values into percentages. The sum is always 100 per cent. So far it is EASY, but what per cent are the remaining amounts? First you will need the numbers with which you calculate.

	Amounts	Per cent
	1000	
	500	
	300	
	2300	
	4500	
Total:		

1 Enter text and numbers.

B *I* U

2 Highlight the text ...

	Amounts	**Per cent**
	1000	
	500	
	300	
	2300	
	4500	
Total:		

3 ... by formatting it with the *Bold* button.

The overview may be an account presentation, cost analysis, and so on. Specify the symbol '£' for the pound sterling currency.

It might also be number of units (for production, on an assembly line, eggs in your hen-house), measuring units (litres of beer or petrol consumption, metres of road construction).

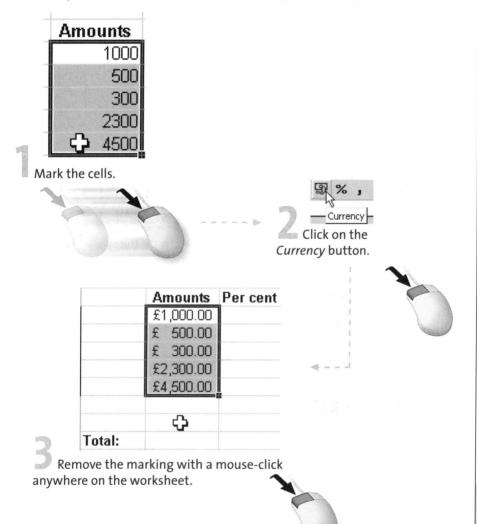

Mark the cells.

Click on the
Currency button.

Remove the marking with a mouse-click
anywhere on the worksheet.

Adding up

To find the per cent values, you need the total, that is the sum of the numbers.

Activate the cell in which you want the result to appear. Click on the *AutoSum* button and Excel marks the cells above with a dotted line.

⏎ Press Enter once and the result is inserted (see Chapter 3).

	Amounts	Per cent
	£1,000.00	
	£ 500.00	
	£ 300.00	
	£2,300.00	
	£4,500.00	
Total:		

1 Click on the cell where you want the result to appear.

2 Activate the *AutoSum* button.

	Amounts	Per cent
	£1,000.00	
	£ 500.00	
	£ 300.00	
	£2,300.00	
	£4,500.00	
Total:	=SUM(B4:B10)	

3 Excel marks the cells with the dotted line.

	Amounts	Per cent
	£1,000.00	
	£500.00	
	£300.00	
	£2,300.00	
	£4,500.00	
Total:	£8,600.00	

4 Confirm with the ⏎Enter key.

Cell names

To establish the individual per cent values, you need the **sum of the individual amounts** (= 100%).

Naming this cell facilitates the whole matter significantly. To assign a **name** to it, a cell has to be activated.

Then simply put the cursor into the *Name box* on the Formula bar. Type the name. This has the advantage that you can always **refer** to the **cell** 'Total' when you are calculating.

	Total	▼		=
		Name Box	B	
1				

	Amounts	Per cent
	£1,000.00	
	£ 500.00	
	£ 300.00	
	£2,300.00	
	£4,500.00	

1 Total: £8,600.0

Click on the cell in which the total '£ 8,600.00' is displayed.

Name box

Total	▼	=	=SUM(B

	A	B	C
1			
2			
3		Amounts	Per cent
4		£1,000.00	
5		£ 500.00	
6		£ 300.00	
7		£2,300.00	
8		£4,500.00	
9			
10			
11	Total:	£8,600.00	

2 Activate the name box, and type 'Total'. Confirm with the Enter key.

191

Per cent values

Now you only have to enter the correct formula to establish the percentage values of the individual numbers. Try to remember what you learnt when you were at school (maybe you are still in school?).

You need the rule of three from your maths lessons. Let's start at the beginning again, asking the question: 'What is the rule of three?'

One per cent is ... ???

Take the result, in the example, of the total of all values: '8,600'.

To find 1 per cent of '8,600' you need to divide '8,600' by '100 %'.

$$1\% = \left(\frac{8.600}{100} \right)$$

£ 1,000 is how much per cent???

$$8.600 - 100\,\%$$
$$1.000 - x\,\%$$

$$X = \frac{100 \times 1000}{8.600}$$

If you want to know what per cent '£ 1,000' is of '£ 8,600', the formula is as shown.

The per cent format

The '1,000' represents the **amount in £.**

The '**8,600**' under the line represent the 'TOTAL'. You have already labelled the cell into which it will be entered.

Amounts	Per cent
£1,000.00	
£ 500.00	
£ 300.00	
£2,300.00	
£4,500.00	

> **CAUTION**
> When you click on the *Percent Style* button, Excel automatically **multiplies** the cell contents by **100.**

On the Formatting toolbar you will find the *Percent Style* button. You need to specify that in one or more cells **per cent values** will be entered.

That means: you do not need to multiply by 100.

The result

Thus, in this example, you only need to divide the amount by the total and then click on the button with the per cent sign (%).

$$?\% = \left(\frac{\text{amount in £}}{\text{Total Amount}} \right)$$

> **CAUTION**
> To determine shares in per cent, you only need to click on the *Percent Style* button and to divide the individual amount by the total amount.

Amounts	Per cent
£1,000.00	
£ 500.00	
£ 300.00	
£2,300.00	
£4,500.00	

1 Activate the appropriate cell.

2 Click on the sign '=' on the
Formula bar to edit the formula.

Amounts	Per cent
£1,000.00	=B4
£ 500.00	

3 Click – as shown – on the cell to
the left.

Amounts	Per cent
£1,000.00	=B4/
£ 500.00	

4 On the keyboard, type in
the backward slash '/' for
division.

	Amounts	Per cent
	£1,000.00	=B4/Total
	£ 500.00	
	£ 300.00	
	£2,300.00	
	£4,500.00	
Total:	£8,600.00	

5 Activate the cell 'Total'.

6 Confirm the
formula.

7 Click on the *Percent Style*
button.

CAUTION

Excel automatically **rounds up/off** per centage values
(here: 11.62 % = 12 %). Thus, occasionally – because of
the rounding up/off – the total result may not be
100 per cent.

Copying formulas

You have found out the per cent value
for one cell. Now you have to
establish the values of the remaining
ones. So far, all calculations refer to
the '£ amount' and the 'Total'.

The formula in the one cell merely
has to be **copied** into the remaining
cells.

	Amounts	Per cent
	£1,000.00	12%
	£ 500.00	6%
	£ 300.00	3%
	£2,300.00	27%
	£4,500.00	52%
Total:	£8,600.00	100%

Move the mouse pointer onto the **fill handle**. When it turns into a
plus (+) drag down while holding down the mouse button.

Amounts	Per cent
£1,000.00	12%
£ 500.00	

1 Position the mouse pointer
on the **fill handle.**

	Amounts	Per cent
	£1,000.00	12%
	£ 500.00	
	£ 300.00	
	£2,300.00	
	£4,500.00	
Total:	£8,600.00	

2 Copy the formula by dragging downwards while pressing the mouse button. Then release the button.

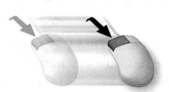

Hiding zero values

You have established all percentage values. Next to the cell 'Total' '100 %' is shown. Everything is correct!

Looking at the calculation there is only one problem: next to the empty rows you can see '0%'. Away with the zeros! Zeros are part of life but sometimes you can do without them!

In Excel you have the option to hide **zeros.**

Choose the TOOLS/OPTIONS menu option. On the *View* tab under *Window options* hide the 'Zero values' by removing the tick in the check box.

	Amounts	Per cent
	£1,000.00	12%
	£ 500.00	6%
	£ 300.00	3%
	£2,300.00	27%
	£4,500.00	52%
		0%
		0%
Total:	£8,600.00	100%

This applies not only to per cent values, but also to all other values.

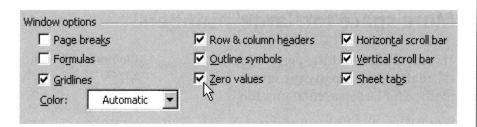

The zeros remain hidden until you choose the same menu and activate 'Zero values' on the *View* tab.

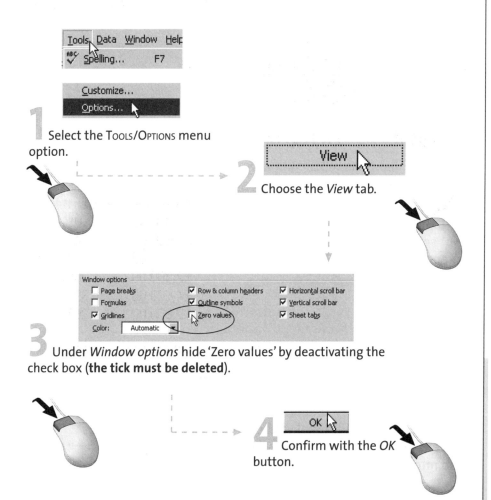

Select the TOOLS/OPTIONS menu option.

Choose the *View* tab.

Under *Window options* hide 'Zero values' by deactivating the check box (**the tick must be deleted**).

Confirm with the *OK* button.

More space for 'large' numbers!

This concludes our little percentage calculation. You can use the same method for larger calculations, too.

When you enter new values, Excel automatically recalculates the new percentages.

	Amounts	Per cent
	£1,000.00	12%
	£ 500.00	6%
	£ 300.00	3%
	£2,300.00	27%
	£4,500.00	52%
Total:	£8,600.00	100%

	£4,500.00
	2800
Total:	£8,600.00

1 Enter a new value and confirm with the ⏎ Enter key.

	Amounts	Per cent
	£1,000.00	9%
	£ 500.00	4%
	£ 300.00	3%
	£2,300.00	20%
	£4,500.00	39%
	£2,800.00	25%
Total:	#########	100%

2 This is what you get.

If you enter an additional value or higher values than in this example, you may just see a sequence of hashes (##########) and no numbers in the 'Total' cell.

Hashes such as these ######## indicate that a column is too narrow to display the cell contents.

These characters do not indicate an error. Because you have entered a further number, there is not enough **space** in the cell 'Total'.

You only need to adjust the width of the cell or the column. Place the mouse pointer on the line between the column headings.

You can adjust the column width by dragging while pressing the mouse button. Or quicker: just **double-click.** Excel automatically adjusts the column width to accommodate the longest – highest – value.

	Amounts	Per cent
	£ 1,000.00	9%
	£ 500.00	4%
	£ 300.00	3%
	£ 2,300.00	20%
	£ 4,500.00	39%
	£ 2,800.00	25%
Total:	£ 11,400.00	100%

	Amounts	Per cent
	£1,000.00	9%
	£ 500.00	4%
	£ 300.00	3%
	£2,300.00	20%
	£4,500.00	39%
	£2,800.00	25%
Total:	########	100%

1 If there is not enough space in a cell (that is, if the cell displays #####), ...

199

ts	Pe
00	
00	
00	
00	
00	
00	
###	

2 ... position the mouse pointer on the line between the column headings.

Amounts	Per cent
£ 1,000.00	9%
£ 500.00	4%
£ 300.00	3%
£ 2,300.00	20%
£ 4,500.00	39%
£ 2,800.00	25%
£ 11,400.00	100%

3 Automatically adjust the column with a double click.

Practise, practise and practise again!

Per cent, per cent, per cent! The Excel coach offers you more exercises for this topic.

Enter the text and numbers. Then:

1) Establish the total number of units.

2) Use the name box to assign the cell name 'Total number of units'.

3) Click on the cell to the right of 'Number of units for Adam'.

Produced Items

	Items	Share in %
Adam	1.234	
Miller	4.555	
Smith	1.025	
Zimmer	3.578	
Edwards	3.323	
Shaw	4.023	
Thompson	4.506	
Black	2.223	

Produced Items

	Items	Share in %
Adam	1.234	5%
Miller	4.555	19%
Smith	1.025	4%
Zimmer	3.578	15%
Edwards	3.323	14%
Shaw	4.023	16%
Thompson	4.506	18%
Black	2.223	9%
	24.467	100%

4) Activate the equal sign for 'edit formula'.

5) Divide the 'number of units' by the 'total number'.

6) Select *Percent Style*.

7) Copy the formula into the cells below.

Enter the text and the numbers for the budget.

Then:

1) Establish the total costs.

2) In the *Name* box assign the cell name 'Costs'.

	Share in £	Share in %
Rent:	£900.00	
Gas & Electric:	£170.00	
Car:	£250.00	
Food:	£520.00	
Miscellaneous:	£320.00	
Total:		

3) Activate the cell to the right of 'Rent/share in £'.

4) Click on the equal sign for 'edit formula'.

5) Divide the cell 'Share in £' by 'Costs'.

	Share in £	Share in %
Rent:	£900.00	42%
Gas & Electric:	£170.00	8%
Car:	£250.00	12%
Food:	£520.00	24%
Miscellaneous:	£320.00	15%
Total:		100%

6) Choose *Percent style*.

7) Copy the formula into the cells below.

8) If necessary, hide the 'zero values' (TOOLS/OPTIONS, *View* tab).

What's in this chapter?

A picture paints a thousand words.
Numbers are easier to digest if they have
been 'embellished' a little. Where facts are
not immediately visible, in Excel charts take
over and are a sight for sore eyes. They are
used to catch the reader's eye and support
your analyses. One glance and everything
is clear. In this way, sober business data are
displayed impressively and need little
further explanation. When the facts
change, it is EASY to change the numbers.
To say it with the words of a famous
German bank:
Peanuts!

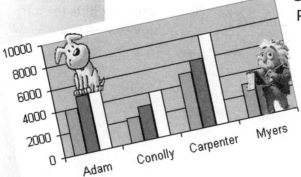

You already know about:

You are going to learn about:

Tables for charts

To avoid those never-ending boring repetitions, Excel offers a quicker entry option. If you wish to enter the NAMES OF MONTHS, you do not need to waste your time entering each one.

You can write the whole word 'January', or choose the abbreviation 'Jan'. You can also use the AutoFill function for the NAMES OF DAYS (see Chapter 7).

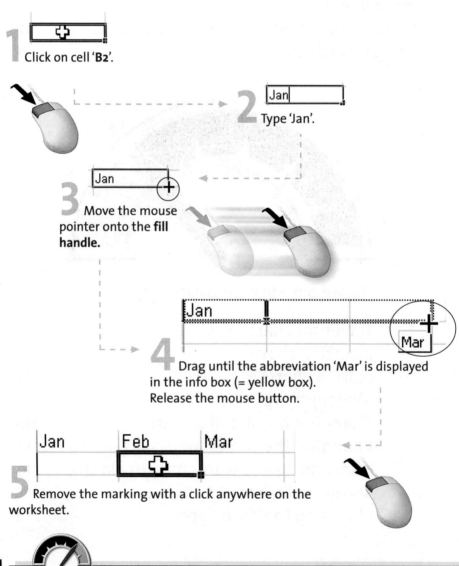

1 Click on cell '**B2**'.

2 Type 'Jan'.

3 Move the mouse pointer onto the **fill handle.**

4 Drag until the abbreviation 'Mar' is displayed in the info box (= yellow box). Release the mouse button.

5 Remove the marking with a click anywhere on the worksheet.

Creating your own custom lists

The lists for months and days are already set up in Excel. However, you can modify or add custom lists.

The Custom LISTS can be found on the Custom Lists *tab under the* TOOLS/OPTIONS *menu command .*

Let's assume you use the same names – such as 'Adam, Miller, Carpenter' – in tables again and again. So why not enter them into a custom list?

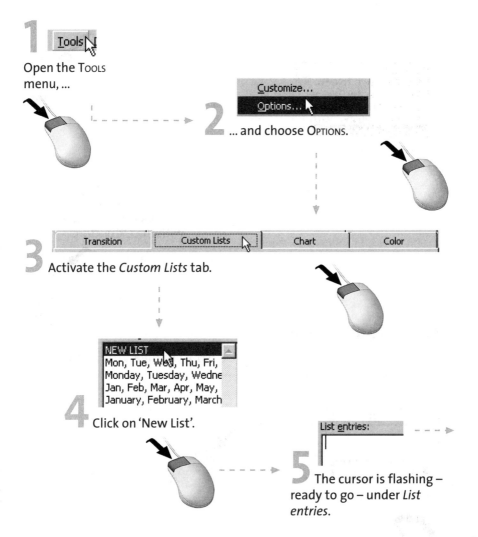

1 Tools

Open the TOOLS menu, ...

2 ... and choose OPTIONS.

Customize...
Options...

3 Activate the *Custom Lists* tab.

Transition | Custom Lists | Chart | Color

4 Click on 'New List'.

NEW LIST
Mon, Tue, Wed, Thu, Fri,
Monday, Tuesday, Wedne
Jan, Feb, Mar, Apr, May,
January, February, March

5 The cursor is flashing – ready to go – under *List entries*.

List entries:

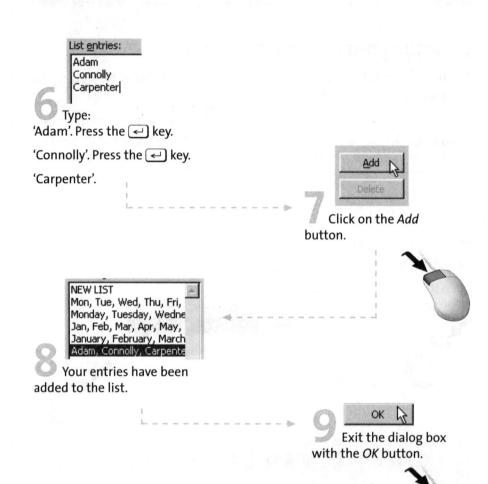

List entries:
Adam
Connolly
Carpenter|

6 Type:

'Adam'. Press the ⏎ key.

'Connolly'. Press the ⏎ key.

'Carpenter'.

7 Click on the *Add* button.

NEW LIST
Mon, Tue, Wed, Thu, Fri,
Monday, Tuesday, Wedne
Jan, Feb, Mar, Apr, May,
January, February, March
Adam, Connolly, Carpente

8 Your entries have been added to the list.

9 Exit the dialog box with the *OK* button.

Inserting your own lists

You have created your own custom list. Now you need to try it out. You must write at least one name.

	A	B
1		
2		Jan
3	⊕	

1 Click on cell '**A3**'.

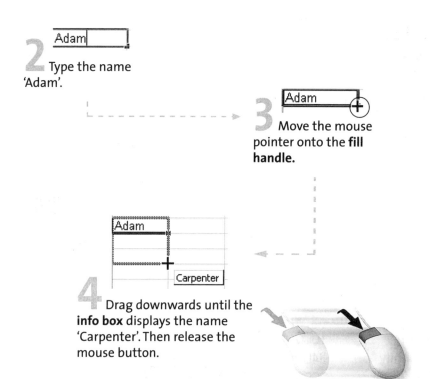

2 Type the name 'Adam'.

3 Move the mouse pointer onto the **fill handle.**

4 Drag downwards until the **info box** displays the name 'Carpenter'. Then release the mouse button.

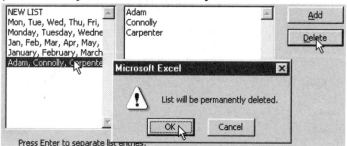

Deleting custom lists

Deleting lists is easy. Again, you need the *Custom Lists* tab (via the TOOLS/OPTIONS menu option).

Simply click on the list you wish to delete and use the Delete button.

You will receive a message informing you that the list will be permanently deleted as soon as you confirm with OK.

NEW LIST
Mon, Tue, Wed, Thu, Fri,
Monday, Tuesday, Wedne
Jan, Feb, Mar, Apr, May,
January, February, March
Adam, Connolly, Carpente

Adam
Connolly
Carpenter

Add

Delete

Microsoft Excel

⚠ List will be permanently deleted.

OK   Cancel

Press Enter to separate list entries.

207

Inserting charts

You wish to add a chart to a brief financial report. You have a vast number of possibilities. It would take more than one chapter to describe all of them.

In the Standard toolbar, you will find the Chart Wizard (you will also find it in Insert/Chart menu). You can start to create you chart as soon as you click on it.

	Jan	Feb	Mar
Adam	1000	5000	2500
Connolly	3400	4000	3500
Carpenter	2000	3000	⟐ 4500

1 Create the table:
'B3': 1000
'B4': 3400
'B5': 2000
'C3': 5000
'C4': 4000
'C5': 3000
'D3': 2500
'D4': 3500
'D5': 4500

| 📊 🔄 | 100% | ▾ | ❓ |

| 🔧 Chart Wizard | 🎨 ▾ |

2 **Click on any cell in the table**. Then start the Chart Wizard with the relevant button.

The Chart Wizard

The **Chart Wizard** appears on your screen.

Chart Wizard - Step 1 of 4 -

The **Chart Wizard** assists you in the creation of charts.

On the Title bar of the dialog box you can see that it goes through four **steps** and you can check at which processing stage you currently are.

Under Chart type *you can choose from various shapes.*

There are columns, lines, pies, bubbles, and so on.

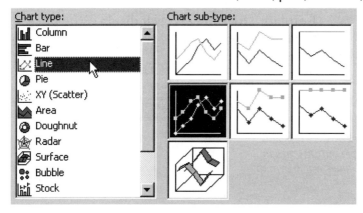

For each type there are in turn Chart sub-types. *For example for* line *you can choose from several variations.*

An overview of some chart types:

Chart type	Application
Column	Compares individual values by means of varying column sizes.
Bar	As column, but the values are displayed on horizontal bars.

209

Chart type	Application
Line	Displays trends and developments over a particular period. These are mainly suited for the display of time-related processes.
Pie	Displays the distribution of the individual data within a whole.
XY (Scatter)	Is used when the values are related (speed: petrol consumption, turnover: costs).
Area	As line chart. It is used to display time-related developments. The extent of the changes is displayed more graphically than in a line chart.
Stock	Useful for 'stockbrokers' as it displays the price fluctuations of shares.

Excel automatically suggests a chart type.

2 Confirm with
the Next *button.*

Which data range?

The second step of the Chart Wizard is to ask you to define the **SERIES**
– in this case 'salesmen' or 'months' – that you wish to include.

Series in rows

When you activate the option Rows, *you will see the monthly
turnovers over one salesman.*

(If you selected the option Columns, *instead, the chart would display
each individual salesmen over one month.)*

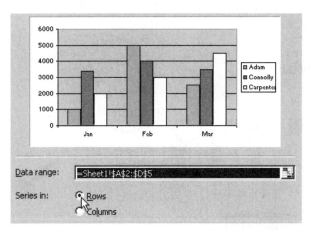

1 *Activate, if necessary, the 'Rows' option under* Series.

2 Let's continue!

Information about the chart

A **legend** provides details about the information areas within a chart.

This is where you specify where you want a **legend** to be added to the chart, as well as other items.

```
☐ Adam
▣ Connolly
☐ Carpenter
```

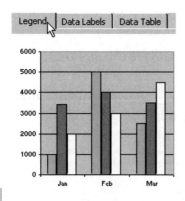

1 Choose the *Legend* tab.

☑ Show legend

Placement

- ● Bottom
- ○ Corner
- ○ Top
- ○ Right
- ○ Left

2 Place the legend at the *Bottom*.

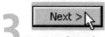
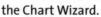
Next >

3 Proceed to the next stage of the Chart Wizard.

Placing the chart

In the last step, you decide where you want the chart to appear. This may be on a separate sheet for large tables.

Since the example table is not very large, integrate the chart on the same sheet.

Which button?

With the *Back* button you can return to the previous steps of the Chart Wizard. There you can – if you so wish – carry out changes.

The *Cancel* button stops the Chart Wizard and you go back to your sheet, as if nothing had happened, without the chart. When you use the *Finish* button, Excel inserts the selected chart.

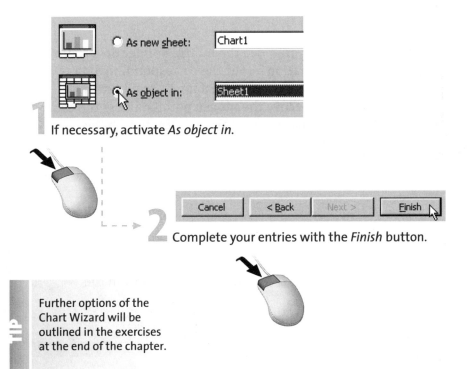

1 If necessary, activate *As object in*.

2 Complete your entries with the *Finish* button.

Further options of the
Chart Wizard will be
outlined in the exercises
at the end of the chapter.

Editing charts

Excel inserts the selected chart into the sheet. To see it you may have to use the scroll bars. When you click on the chart, small black

squares appear. They indicate the size of the chart.

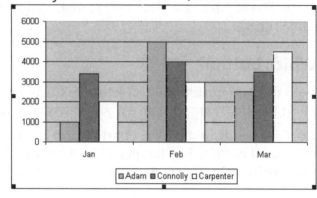

To edit a chart you need to click on it.

Only when the squares are visible is it possible to edit the chart.

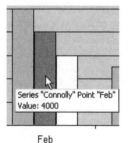

Series "Connolly" Point "Feb"
Value: 4000

Feb

When you move the mouse pointer on a column, **information** about the corresponding data is displayed. (Here: Salesman Connolly, turnover 4000). Move the mouse pointer across the chart and have a look at the information that is displayed.

Moving charts

You can move the chart from one point to another within the worksheet.

Place the mouse pointer within the image. The info box displays **'Chart Area'**.

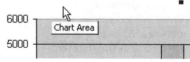

When you press and hold the left mouse button, the mouse pointer turns into a cross hair.

Holding down the mouse button place the chart where you want it on the sheet.

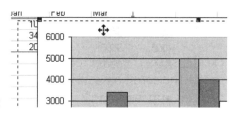

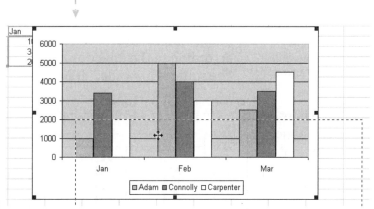

1 Place the mouse pointer within the chart, until the info box displays **Chart Area**.

2 Hold down the left mouse button. **Drag** the chart ...

215

Feb	Mar		
5000	2500		
4000	3500		
3000	4500		
6000			
5000			

3 ... to a place where you can see both – table and chart – better.

Changing the size of a chart

With the drag point of the chart, you can change the size of the chart analagously to the direction of the arrow while pressing the mouse button.

When you move the mouse pointer on the black squares at the edge of the image, you can resize the chart according to the direction of the arrows. The squares are called **drag points.**

In this example, choose the bottom right-hand drag point. To get to it you may have to use the scroll bar, holding down the left mouse button, you can change the size of the chart.

Only if you place the mouse pointer exactly on a drag point can you enlarge or reduce the chart.

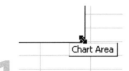

1 Place the mouse pointer onto the drag point.

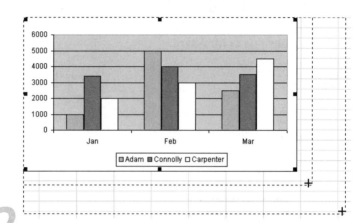

2 Reduce or enlarge the chart according to your own judgement.

Changing the values for a chart

When you double-click on the chart, Excel marks the corresponding table with a coloured outline. The program thus indicates that the image refers to these values. However, you can also edit the individual entries from here.

Example:

Mr Adam is getting very agitated. He has made a mistake when entering the turnover values for January. He has entered £ 4,000 instead of £ 1,000.

217

To add numbers to a diagram you do not need to create a completely new one. You can simply change the corresponding number in the table. Excel automatically adjusts the chart – here: column.

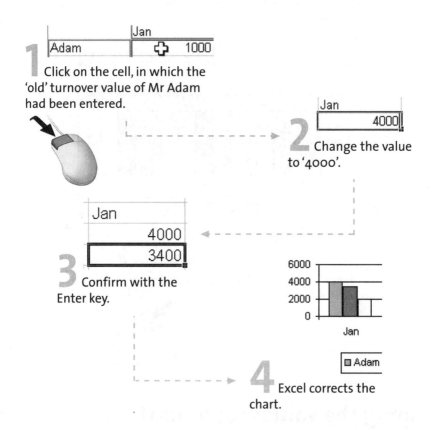

1 Click on the cell, in which the 'old' turnover value of Mr Adam had been entered.

2 Change the value to '4000'.

3 Confirm with the Enter key.

4 Excel corrects the chart.

As you can see, Excel immediately works with the new value.

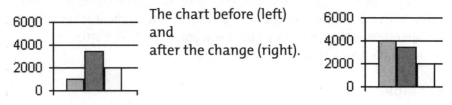

The chart before (left) and after the change (right).

Mr Adam's column grew from £ 1,000 to £ 4,000.

You can also do this the other way round. You can change the numbers within a chart. Click on the appropriate column. Holding down the mouse button, drag the turnover upwards. Excel will automatically adjust the value in the table.

Inserting new features into an old chart

Surely you will get turnover values for more than three months. The new values for April are available now.

Use the **AutoFill function**. Click on 'Mar' and drag the fill handle into the next cell.

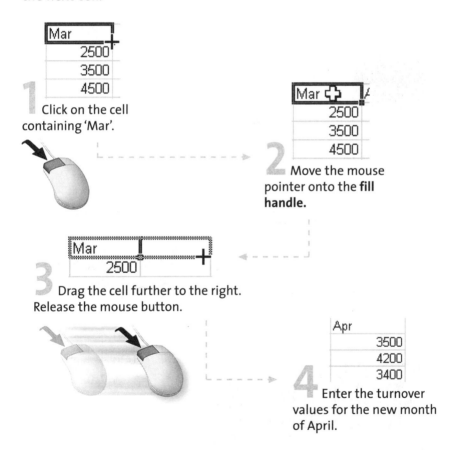

Click on the cell containing 'Mar'.

Move the mouse pointer onto the **fill handle.**

Drag the cell further to the right. Release the mouse button.

Enter the turnover values for the new month of April.

219

New turnover values are available. Do you have to create a new chart? No! Simply drag the new information into the image.

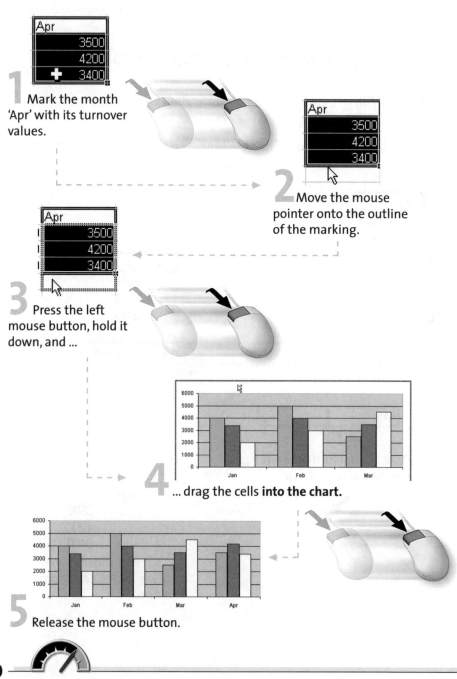

1 Mark the month 'Apr' with its turnover values.

2 Move the mouse pointer onto the outline of the marking.

3 Press the left mouse button, hold it down, and ...

4 ... drag the cells **into the chart**.

5 Release the mouse button.

A new salesman

Just as you can add 'a new month', you can also add a new salesman. First enter the data, mark it, and then with the left mouse button drag the entries into the chart.

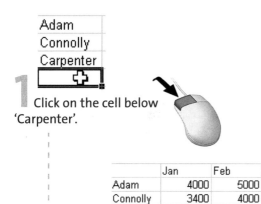

1 Click on the cell below 'Carpenter'.

	Jan	Feb	Mar	Apr
Adam	4000	5000	2500	3500
Connolly	3400	4000	3500	4200
Carpenter	2000	3000	4500	3400
Myers				2300

2 Type in the new data of Mr 'Myers'.

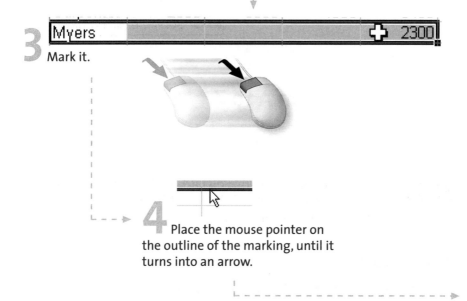

3 Mark it.

4 Place the mouse pointer on the outline of the marking, until it turns into an arrow.

221

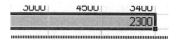

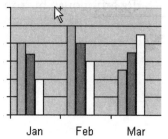

Jan   Feb   Mar

5 Holding down the left mouse button drag into the chart. Then release the mouse button.

A salesman is born! In the same way you can carry on adding to your table and thus to the chart over and over and over again.

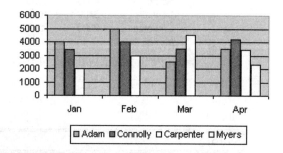

Sorting cells from A to Z

Adding new salesmen may cause some chaos. The list is no longer ordered from A to Z.

On the Standard toolbar, you can see the corresponding buttons. The AZ button sorts the list in **ascending order***, and ZA in* **descending order.**

From A to Z

Mark the whole table, to tell Excel that you wish to sort it.

Adam	4000	5000	2500	3500
Connolly	3400	4000	3500	4200
Carpenter	2000	3000	4500	3400
Myers				2300

1 Mark the table.

2 *Click on the* Ascending *button.*

Sort Ascending

	Jan	Feb	Mar	Apr
Adam	4000	5000	2500	3500
Carpenter	2000	3000	4500	3400
Connolly	3400	4000	3500	4200
Myers				2300

3 The table and ...

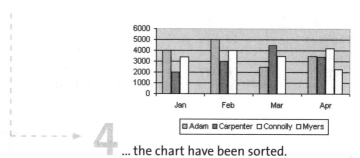

□ Adam ■ Carpenter □ Connolly □ Myers

4 ... the chart have been sorted.

The corresponding turnover values and persons have been taken into account, too.

Changing the chart type

To execute the CHART/CHART TYPE menu option, you need to make sure that the **image** is **active**, that is the drag points must be visible.

If you want to **change** the chart **type** (column, bar, pie), select CHART TYPE in the CHART menu.

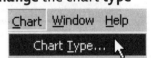

Practise, practise and practise again!

Calculate the percentage components of ingredients in food items. (Tip: it is not beer!) The exercise shows you a few new methods for creating charts. The chart type is a pie. The shares are displayed as percentage values.

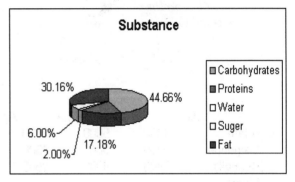

Substance

30.16%	
6.00%	44.66%
2.00%	17.18%

- ■ Carbohydrates
- ■ Proteins
- □ Water
- □ Suger
- ■ Fat

Carbohydrates	44.66%
Proteins	17.18%
Water	2.00%
Suger	6.00%
Fat	30.16%

1 Create a new workbook and create the table as shown.

Carbohydrates	44.66%
Proteins	17.18%
Water	2.00%
Suger	6.00%
Fat	30.16%

2 If necessary, click on a cell within the table.

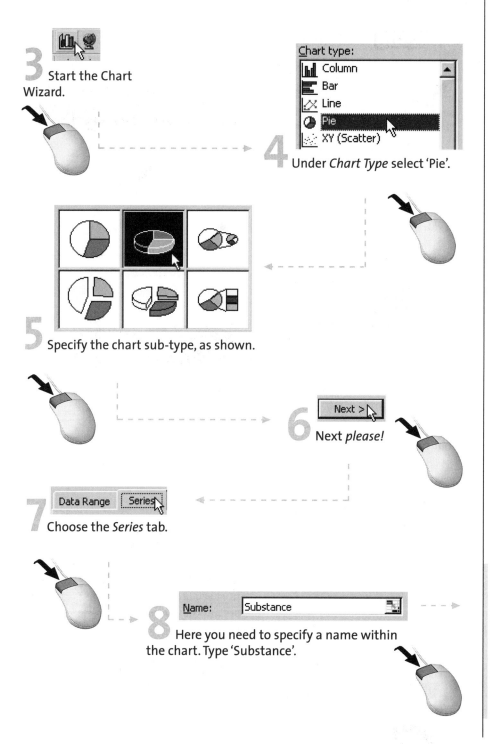

3 Start the Chart Wizard.

4 Under *Chart Type* select 'Pie'.

5 Specify the chart sub-type, as shown.

6 Next *please!*

7 Choose the *Series* tab.

8 Here you need to specify a name within the chart. Type 'Substance'.

9 What *Next*?

10 Activate the *Data Labels* tab .

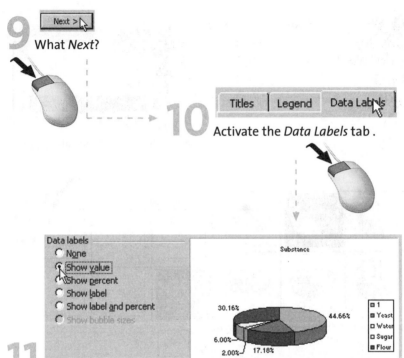

11 If you had not specified per cent in the table, you could activate *Show percent* under *Data labels*. In this exercise choose *Show value*.

Tip: try out the individual options. The Preview window shows you what these look like.

12 You do not need to go through all the steps of the Chart Wizard in this example, and thus can finish your entries here.

Would you like to create more charts? **Go through the sub-steps independently**. If necessary create a new workbook.

	Cost	Turnover
January	2300	1500
February	2100	1900
March	1800	2300
April	1700	2700

1 Type in the shown worksheet.

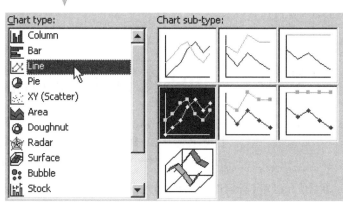

2 Select the 'Line' chart type.

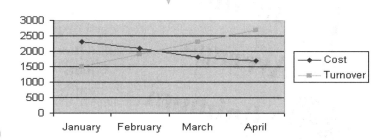

3 Move and enlarge the chart.

227

What's in this chapter?

There are people who draw up statistics for just about everything. What are statistics?

Statistics are, for instance, when a man drinks three bottles of wine in a restaurant. This is of no help to you and me.

However, according to statistics, the man, you and I have each drunk a bottle of wine.

Cheers – to your health!

Maximum

Average

Minimum

You already know about:

You are going to learn about:

Inserting functions

Who has the highest and who the lowest turnover? In Excel you can also carry out statistical analyses.

In this chapter we take as an example football clubs and goals. Of course, you can use the same method in other areas: production, sales, cost analyses, and so on.

First enter the clubs.

CAUTION

If there is too little space in a column, automatically adjust the column width.

If your favourite club is not included, feel free to enter it, too. The procedure will not be affected by a new name.

Move the mouse pointer onto the line between the column headings and double-click. Excel automatically adjusts the column width to accommodate the longest entry.

Football Club	No. of Goals
Arsenal	
Bolton	
Manchester United	
Sheffield Wednesday	
Leeds United	
Newcastle	
Liverpool	

1 Enter the clubs.

2 Adjust the width of the column by double-clicking on the line between the column headings.

Football Club	No. of Goals		Statistics
Arsenal			Highest No. of goals
Bolton			Lowest No. of goals
Manchester United			Average
Sheffield Wednesday			
Leeds United			Total No. of clubs
Newcastle			More than 20 Goals scored
Liverpool			

3 Long live statistics! Enter the additional text.

Football Club	No. of Goals		Statistics
Arsenal	29		Highest No. of goals
Bolton	19		Lowest No. of goals
Manchester United	21		Average
Sheffield Wednesday	30		
Leeds United	29		Total No. of clubs
Newcastle	30		More than 20 Goals scored
Liverpool	34		

4 Goal, goal, goal! No goal statistics without goals!

One name for several cells

In this example, for any further work with Excel, it makes sense to name the cell range that is to be analysed. In this case this is the goal area. Call it 'Goals'. This will facilitate the matter later! Thus, in your statistical analysis you only need to specify 'Goals' and no cell range.

Mark the **cell range,** click on the *Name* box, and enter the name.

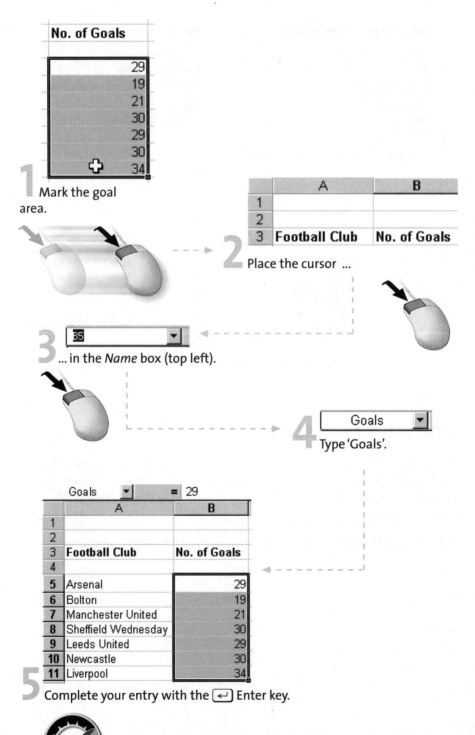

No. of Goals

	29
	19
	21
	30
	29
	30
	34

1 Mark the goal area.

	A	B
1		
2		
3	**Football Club**	**No. of Goals**

2 Place the cursor ...

35

3 ... in the *Name* box (top left).

Goals

4 Type 'Goals'.

Goals = 29

	A	B
1		
2		
3	**Football Club**	**No. of Goals**
4		
5	Arsenal	29
6	Bolton	19
7	Manchester United	21
8	Sheffield Wednesday	30
9	Leeds United	29
10	Newcastle	30
11	Liverpool	34

5 Complete your entry with the ↵ Enter key.

Why use functions?

In Excel various functions are available to you.

A function is a pre-set formula. A formula carries out particular calculations in the respective cells.

First, the highest number of goals needs to be established. Instead of 'highest number' you can say 'maximum'. Thus, the function you need is called MAX in Excel.

All functions are located in the FUNCTION WIZARD. You can call it up with the *Paste Function* button on the Standard toolbar. The Function wizard helps you to insert functions.

In the following dialog box, you can choose from the items under *Function category*.

At the very top you can see *Last used*. Here you will find the functions with which you have **worked most recently.** (Unfortunately this does not apply to you yet!) As soon as you have used MAX, you can also call up this function here.

All functions are listed under *All*. Thus, you can always use this category.

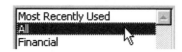

Then categories such as 'Financial, Date &

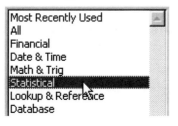

Time, Math & Trig' follow.

Depending on the effect of a function, you can also find it in individual subject categories.

Unfortunately, you will not always know which category a function belongs to. The function MAX is listed under the category 'Statistical'.

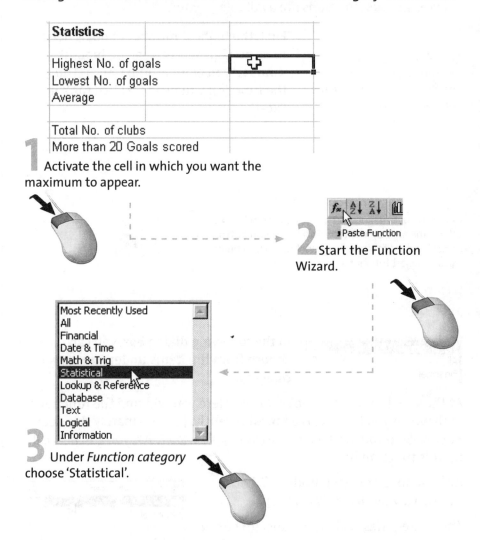

Statistics		
Highest No. of goals		⊕
Lowest No. of goals		
Average		
Total No. of clubs		
More than 20 Goals scored		

1 Activate the cell in which you want the maximum to appear.

*f*ₓ ▯ Paste Function

2 Start the Function Wizard.

Most Recently Used
All
Financial
Date & Time
Math & Trig
Statistical
Lookup & Reference
Database
Text
Logical
Information

3 Under *Function category* choose 'Statistical'.

When you have chosen a category, concentrate on choosing the correct function.

There are many. You can scroll through them with the scroll bar. However, there is an easier way!

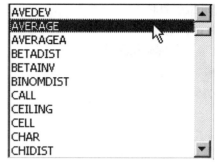

TIP

To find a function faster, simply enter its INITIAL LETTER.

When you click on the first function you will notice a yellow dotted line.

The function MAX begins with the letter 'M'.

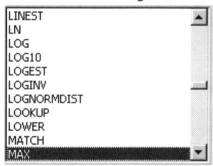

When you type the letter 'm' (capitalisation is not important here) on the keyboard, the blue marking under FUNCTION NAME automatically jumps to the first expression which begins with 'M'. Coincidentally this is MAX, which you need in this example.

CAUTION

You cannot enter a second letter. If you, for example entered 'A', Excel would jump back to the functions which begin with an 'A'.

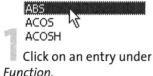

1 Click on an entry under *Function*.

235

```
LOOKUP
LOWER
MATCH
MAX
```

2 On the keyboard,
type the letter 'm'.

In addition, in the dialog box you will
find information about what the
respective function does. In this case, the
DESCRIPTION of the Maximum) function.

MAX(number1,number2,...)

Returns the largest value in a set of values. Ignores logical values and text.

The maximum

Here you start the function by double clicking.

The entry box appears. Under *Number1* specify the **range** for which
the maximum has to be found. In this case: 'Goals'.

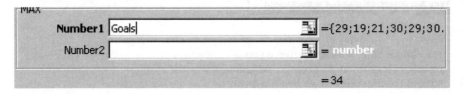

```
MAX
   Number1  Goals                              ={29;19;21;30;29;30.
   Number2                                     = number
                                               = 34
```

You already know the result in advance. Here it is '34'. With the button
OK the result of the function is integrated in the worksheet.

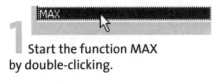

1 Start the function MAX
by double-clicking.

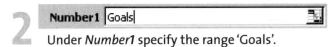

2 Under *Number1* specify the range 'Goals'.

3 Complete your entries.

Excel inserts the highest value of the selected cell range.

Highest No. of goals	34
Lowest No. of goals	
Average	
Total No. of clubs	
More than 20 Goals scored	

On the **Formula bar** you can see the formula: 'MAX(Goals)'.

= =MAX(Goals)

In layman's terms this means: this is the maximum for the 'Goals' cell range.

The minimum

Where there is a maximum, there is also a minimum. You wish to find the lowest number of goals. The procedure is almost the same as for finding the maximum.

| Highest No. of goals | 34 |
| Lowest No. of goals | |

1 Activate the cell in which you want the minimum to appear.

2 Start the Function Wizard.

237

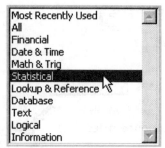

3 If necessary, select 'Statistical'
under *Function Category*.

Click on any function and type the letter 'm' on the keyboard. Excel
jumps to the first function which begins with 'M'. It is MAX. You do
not need this function, but you need MIN for minimum instead.

If you entered 'i' for the second letter, the functions beginning with 'I'
would be shown. You do not want that to happen!

Simply scroll downwards a little using the scroll bar or press the
⬇Arrow down key until the function MIN is displayed.

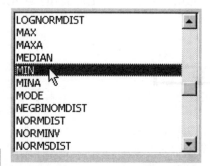

1 Select MIN, and start the function by
double-clicking.

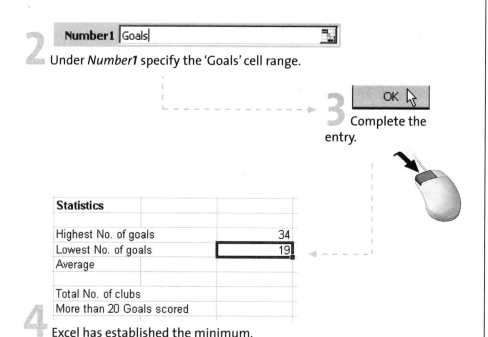

2 Under *Number1* specify the 'Goals' cell range.

3 Complete the entry.

Statistics	
Highest No. of goals	34
Lowest No. of goals	19
Average	
Total No. of clubs	
More than 20 Goals scored	

4 Excel has established the minimum.

How are you? Average!

In the next cell the average number of goals needs to be established. The procedure is again the same as for maximum and minimum.

The term for average' in statistics is mean.

Statistics	
Highest No. of goals	34
Lowest No. of goals	19
Average	

1 Click on the appropriate cell.

2 Activate the *Paste function* button.

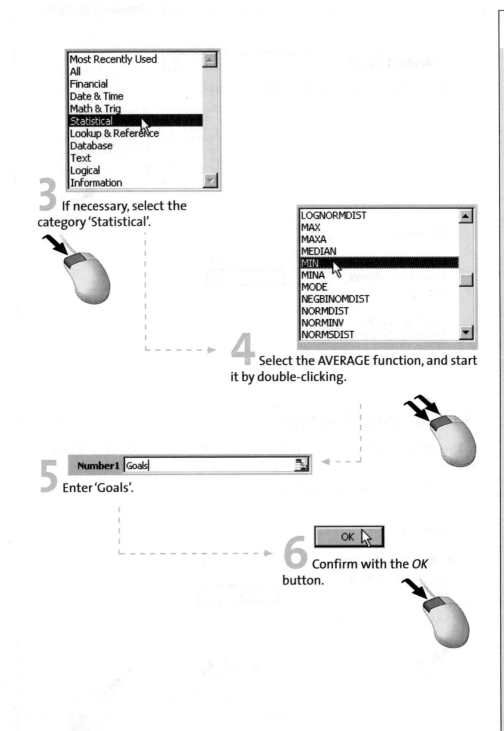

Most Recently Used
All
Financial
Date & Time
Math & Trig
Statistical
Lookup & Reference
Database
Text
Logical
Information

3 If necessary, select the category 'Statistical'.

LOGNORMDIST
MAX
MAXA
MEDIAN
MIN
MINA
MODE
NEGBINOMDIST
NORMDIST
NORMINV
NORMSDIST

4 Select the AVERAGE function, and start it by double-clicking.

5 Number1 | Goals

Enter 'Goals'.

OK

6 Confirm with the *OK* button.

Numbers with decimal values

When calculating averages, the established value may have **decimal places**. You can remove them one by one with the *Decrease Decimal* button.
One mouse-click removes one decimal place. **Excel rounds up/off** accordingly.

Statistics		
Highest No. of goals		34
Lowest No. of goals		19
Average		27.4285714
Total No. of clubs		
More than 20 Goals scored		

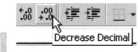

1 Click on the *Decrease Decimal* button, ...

2 ... and remove the *decimal places*, until you have the number '27'.

If you, on the other hand, wish to add decimal places, operate the *Increase decimal* button.

Calculating with functions

The COUNT function only counts cells that contain numbers. In contrast COUNTA counts all cells that are not empty – regardless of whether they contain text or numbers.

With the COUNTA function you can establish how many clubs are entered. You have the additional option to choose 'Count'.

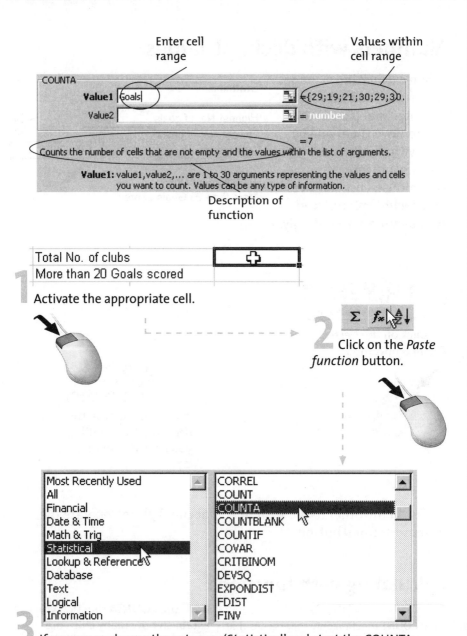

Enter cell range

Values within cell range

COUNTA

Value1 Goals = {29;19;21;30;29;30.

Value2 = number

= 7

Counts the number of cells that are not empty and the values within the list of arguments.

Value1: value1,value2,... are 1 to 30 arguments representing the values and cells you want to count. Values can be any type of information.

Description of function

| Total No. of clubs | ✚ |
| More than 20 Goals scored | |

1 Activate the appropriate cell.

Σ f_x ₂↓

2 Click on the *Paste function* button.

Most Recently Used	CORREL
All	COUNT
Financial	COUNTA
Date & Time	COUNTBLANK
Math & Trig	COUNTIF
Statistical	COVAR
Lookup & Reference	CRITBINOM
Database	DEVSQ
Text	EXPONDIST
Logical	FDIST
Information	FINV

3 If necessary, choose the category 'Statistical' and start the COUNTA function with a double click.

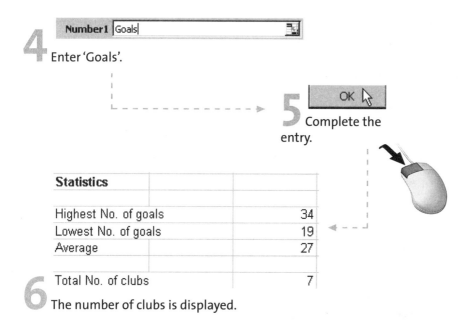

4 Enter 'Goals'.

5 Complete the entry.

Statistics	
Highest No. of goals	34
Lowest No. of goals	19
Average	27
Total No. of clubs	7

6 The number of clubs is displayed.

The COUNTIF function

If only! In this example the entry will be slightly more specific.

You are looking for instances where the number of goals is greater than '20'. Excel is supposed to count only the instances which fulfil this criterion.

Here you use the same procedure that you already know from the other functions. The range is still the same ('Goals'). Under *Search* enter '>20'. Excel counts all cells, which contain numbers bigger than '20' (that is 21, 22, 23, ...).

COUNTIF		
Range	Goals	={29;19;21;30;29;30.
Criteria	>20	=

=

Counts the number of cells within a range that meet the given condition.

Criteria is the condition in the form of a number, expression, or text that defines which cells will be counted.

This is an overview of the signs used for the various search options (with the example value '20'):

SEARCH CRITERION	SIGN	RESULT
More than '20'	>20	21, 22, 23, ...
More or equal '20'	>=20	20, 21, 22, ...
Less than '20'	<20	19, 18, 17, ...
Less or equal '20'	<=20	20, 19, 18, ...

Statistics		
Highest No. of goals		34
Lowest No. of goals		19
Average		27
Total No. of clubs		7
More than 20 Goals scored		

1 Click on the appropriate cell.

2 Start the *Function Wizard*.

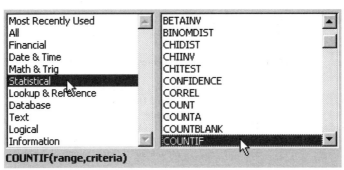

COUNTIF(range,criteria)

If necessary, select the category 'Statistical'. Enter the COUNTIF function and start it with a double click.

Range Goals

The range to be analysed is 'Goals'.

Criteria >20

Under *Search* enter '>20'.

OK

Complete your entry.

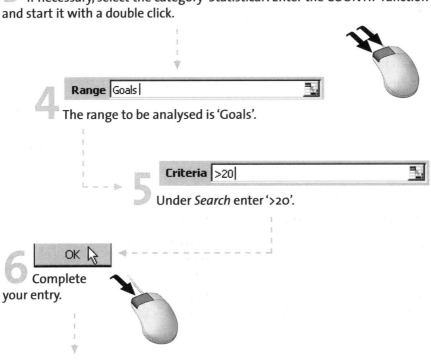

Football Club	No. of Goals		Statistics		
Arsenal	29		Highest No. of goals		34
Bolton	19		Lowest No. of goals		19
Manchester United	21		Average		27
Sheffield Wednesday	30				
Leeds United	29		Total No. of clubs		7
Newcastle	30		More than 20 Goals scored		6
Liverpool	34				

The number of clubs that scored more than 20 goals.

Changing a formula

Football Club	No. of Goals		Statistics		
Arsenal	29		Highest No. of goals		34
Bolton	19		Lowest No. of goals		19
Manchester United	21		Average		27
Sheffield Wednesday	30				
Leeds United	29		Total No. of clubs		7
Newcastle	30		More than 20 Goals scored		6
Liverpool	34				

This concludes our small statistical analysis.

After each new round of matches you simply change the numbers.

You will notice how the statistics are automatically recalculated. Changing an entry is thus incredibly *easy*. Take the function COUNTIF for example.

Click on the corresponding cell and you can see the formula in the Formula bar.

When you double-click on it, Excel indicates in blue script the rangefrom which the analyses are taken.

Football Club	No. of Goals		Statistics		
Arsenal	29		Highest No. of goals		34
Bolton	19		Lowest No. of goals		19
Manchester United	21		Average		27
Sheffield Wednesday	30				
Leeds United	29		Total No. of clubs		7
Newcastle	30		More than 20 Goals scored		6
Liverpool	34				

So far it was 'COUNTIF (Goals">20")'. Change it to '>30'.

You do not need to start the Function Wizard, but can implement the changes in the FORMULA BAR. Replace the '2' with a '3'.

= =COUNTIF(Goals,">20")

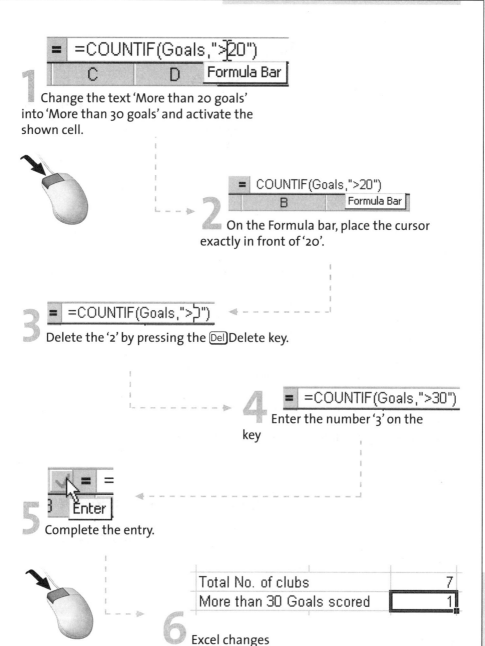

1 =COUNTIF(Goals,">20")

| C | D | Formula Bar |

Change the text 'More than 20 goals' into 'More than 30 goals' and activate the shown cell.

2 COUNTIF(Goals,">20")

| B | Formula Bar |

On the Formula bar, place the cursor exactly in front of '20'.

3 =COUNTIF(Goals,">0")

Delete the '2' by pressing the [Del]Delete key.

4 =COUNTIF(Goals,">30")

Enter the number '3' on the key

5 Enter

Complete the entry.

| Total No. of clubs | 7 |
| More than 30 Goals scored | 1 |

6 Excel changes the value.

A different way – the same goal

To insert formulas you do not need to enter the data in the Function Wizard. You also do not need to name cell ranges here.

Statistics		
Highest No. of goals		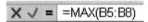
Lowest No. of goals		
Average		

X ✓ = | =MAX(B5:B8)

Let's assume you had to reanalyse the statistics! Again the maximum, that is the function MAX, is specified.

Click on the cell, start the Function Wizard as usual, and activate the function MAX.

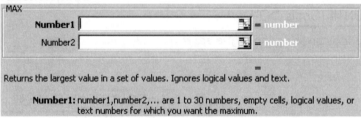

MAX

Number1 | | = number

Number2 | | = number

=

Returns the largest value in a set of values. Ignores logical values and text.

Number1: number1,number2,... are 1 to 30 numbers, empty cells, logical values, or text numbers for which you want the maximum.

Do not make any entries, but **immediately** confirm with the *OK* button.

Excel shows an ERROR MESSAGE. Do not pay any attention to it. When you click on the *OK* button, Excel inserts PART OF THE FORMULA.

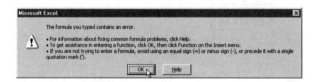

 Only the specification 'cells to be analysed' is missing. The **cursor** is flashing between the **brackets** ( ).

No. of Goals
31
23
24
32
32
31
38

4R x 1C

Holding down the mouse button, specify the **range** you wish to choose. You will notice a dotted line around the cells.

Once you have included all cells, confirm the formula.

This procedure works for all formulas, and not only for MAX.

A loan calculation

You can also find useful functions in other categories.

Example:

You wish to calculate the monthly repayment on a loan. The loan amount is 20,000 euros. The interest rate is 9 per cent. You are going to pay it back within four years (48 months).

1 Open a new workbook.

	A	B
1	Mortgage	
2		
3	Amount	20000
4	Interest	9%
5	No. of payments	48
6		
7	Payment	

2 Enter the data into the appropriate cells.

Payment

3 The monthly repayment is going to appear in cell B7. Activate the cell with a mouse click.

Σ *f*≈ ₂↓ Z↓

4 Click on the *Paste Function* button.

Most Recently Used
All
Financial
Date & Time

5 Select the *Financial* function category.

Function name:

DB
DDB
FV
IPMT
IRR
ISPMT
MIRR
NPER
NPV
PMT
PPMT

6 With the scroll bar (located to the right under *Function name)* scroll until you can see the *PMT* item.

7

| Rate | B4| | | = 0.09 |

Double-click on *PMT*.

8

| Rate | B4 | | = 0.09 |
| Nper | B5| | = 48 |

Specify cell 'B4' (= represents the interest rate). Press the
⇧Tab key.

9

Rate	B4		= 0.09
Nper	B5		= 48
Pv	B3		= 20 000

Type the cell name 'B5' (= number of payments). Confirm with the Tab
key.

10

| OK |

At this point you
need to specify cell 'B3'
(= loan amount).

Changing the function with the Formula bar

However, this small calculation has two flaws!

You wanted to know the monthly and not the yearly payments! The 9 per cent interest rate (in cell B4) is a yearly rate. You must divide it by 12 months.

You can carry out these small modifications in the **Formula bar.**

| B7 | ▼ | | = | RMZ(B4;B5;B3) |

	A	B	C
1	Mortgage		
2			
3	Amount	20000	
4	Interest	9%	
5	No. of payments	48	
6			
7	Payment	(£1,829.23)	

1 | **=** | =RMZ(B4

If necessary click on cell 'B7' and on the Formula bar exactly **after** 'B4' and before the semicolon ';'.

2 | **=** | =RMZ(B4/

Enter the backward slash '/' for **division** on the keyboard.

3 | **=** | =RMZ(B4/12

Type in the number '12'.

4 | ⬚ **=** | =RMZ(B4/12;B5;B3)

Confirm the formula.

Changing the function with the Function Wizard

The second flaw is that the loan amount is shown with a minus sign on your

Payment	(£497.70)

spreadsheet. Admittedly, paying out money is always a negative thing, but this fact of life is not relevant in this example.

When you click on a cell containing a formula, and then on the equal sign (=) on the Formula bar, you immediately get into the relevant dialog box.

This time you are going to carry out the modifications with the **Function Wizard** without starting it.

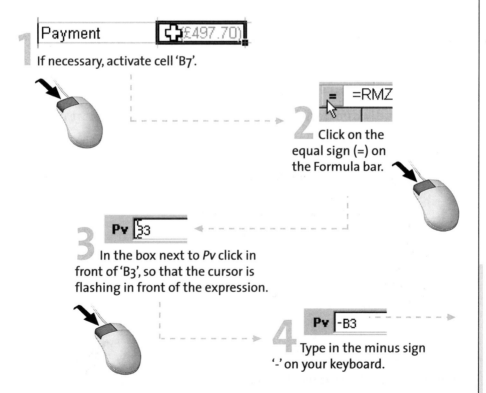

1 If necessary, activate cell 'B7'.

2 Click on the equal sign (=) on the Formula bar.

3 In the box next to *Pv* click in front of 'B3', so that the cursor is flashing in front of the expression.

4 Type in the minus sign '-' on your keyboard.

Formula result = £164,228.35   [OK]

5 Confirm the formula with the *OK* button.

	A	B
1	Mortgage	
2		
3	Amount	20000
4	Interest	9%
5	No. of payments	48
6		
7	Payment	£497.70

Practise, practise and practise again!

There is more to analyse than just goals. First you are going to create an overview on your worksheet.

Enter the individual formulas with the Function Wizard. Start it using the appropriate button.

			Turnover in £
	January		
Adam		March	
Miller			
Smith			
Zimmer			
Edwards			
Shaw			
Thompson			

1 Create a new workbook. Enter the text into the cells, and specify with the help of the AutoFill function the months 'January', 'February' and 'March'.

		Turnover in £	
	January	February	March
Adam	1,500	2,450	9,200
Miller	2,300	5,000	5,800
Smith	4,500	3,100	7,000
Zimmer	5,600	3,400	5,600
Edwards	11,000	2,750	8,900
Shaw	13,000	4,300	7,800
Thompson	500	4,200	12,000

2 Enter the turnover values.

Highest Turnover	
Lowest Turnover	
Average Turnover	
Turnover £	1,000.00
Turnover £	5,000.00

3 Enter the criteria for the individual analyses as shown.

		Turnover in £	
	January	February	March
Adam	1,500	2,450	9,200
Miller	2,300	5,000	5,800
Smith	4,500	3,100	7,000
Zimmer	5,600	3,400	5,600
Edwards	11,000	2,750	8,900
Shaw	13,000	4,300	7,800
Thompson	500	4,200	12,000

4 Mark the turnover values, and ...

Turnover	▼	=	1500	
	A	B	C
1			
2			
3		January	February
4	Adam	1,500	2,450
5	Miller	2,300	5,000

5 ... assign the name 'Turnover' to the marked cell range.

255

Turnover	▼	=	1500

	A	B	C
1			
2			
3		January	February
4	Adam	1,500	2,45
5	Miller	2,300	5,00

6 Confirm with the [↵] Enter key.

---MAX---

Number1	Turnover|	📊	={1500,2450,9200;2:
Number2		📊	= number

7 Establish the highest turnover.

---MIN---

Number1	Turnover|	📊	={1500,2450,6200;2:
Number2		📊	= number

8 What is the lowest turnover?

---AVERAGE---

Number1	Turnover|	📊	={1500,2450,9200;2:
Number2		📊	= number

9 How much is the average turnover?

---COUNTIF---

Range	Turnover	📊	={1500,2450,9200;2:
Criteria	>1,000|	📊	=

10 How many turnover values are there over £1,000?

COUNTIF
| Range | Turnover | | ={1500,2450,9200;2: |
| Criteria | >5,000 | | = |

11 How many turnover values are there over £5,000?

Highest Turnover	13000
Lowest Turnover	500
Average Turnover	5710
Turnover £ 1,000.00	20
Turnover £ 5,000.00	10

12 These are the provisional results.

13 Turnover £ 1,000.00

Change the text 'Turnover over £1000'
into ... '£2000'.

| ⊕ | 20 |

14 By pressing the ⟨⇥⟩ Tab key move one cell to the right.

15 With the equal sign (=) on the Formula bar change ...

COUNTIF
| Range | Turnover |
| Criteria | >2,000 |

16 ... the criterion accordingly. Then complete your entry with the *OK* button.

Change a few turnover values!

What's in this chapter?

Money, money, money. When you look into your wallet, what do you see? Nothing!?! 'But yesterday it was still full!' You wonder and rub your eyes. Where has it all gone? Forget the mess. With an easy-to-understand cashbook you can always keep track of what you have spent your money on. Compare your income and your expenses, and work out your current cash balance. Excel automatically adds or subtracts the amount and not only once, but daily, monthly, or yearly.

| | | | Income | £1,290.00 | |
| | | | Expenses | =SUM(E9:E17) | |

			£200.00	
			£950.10	

Balance C/O
Final cash balance

		Income	Expenses	Cash
				£400.00
		£200.00		£320.00
Serial No	Text		£80.00	£120.00
1	Cheque		£200.00	£90.05
2	Stamps		£29.95	£205.05
3	Petty cash			£5.05
4	Excel EASY	£115.00	£200.00	£405.05
5	Cash Payment			£980.05
6	Cash (Private)	£400.00		£950.10
7	Cheque	£575.00	£29.95	
8	Cash payment			9R x 1C
9	Word EASY			
10	Final cash balance			

You already know about:

You are going to learn about:

Inserting functions

First decide as to what you are going to do. You are going to design a 'cashbook' and the word should appear on your worksheet.
Highlight the expression 'cashbook' by choosing a different **Font Size**.

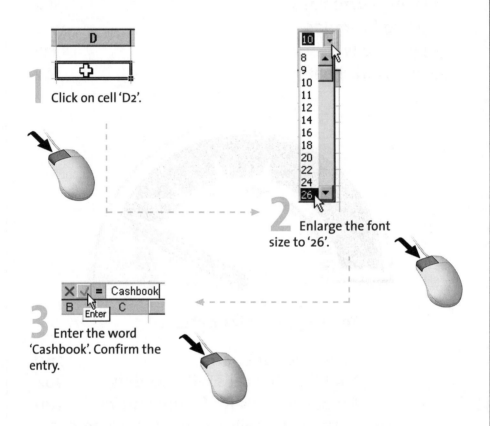

1 Click on cell 'D2'.

2 Enlarge the font size to '26'.

3 Enter the word 'Cashbook'. Confirm the entry.

The structure of the cashbook

What should the cashbook display? Excel can calculate the individual VAT amounts. Furthermore, the receipt date can be recorded.

We are only going to compare **income** and **expenses** for reasons of clarity in this chapter. Otherwise you, as a beginner, 'will not see the wood for the trees'. In the end, the structure of your cashbook is up to you! In this chapter you only create its general framework. Later you can set up your cashbook according to your personal requirements.

In this example you are also going to calculate your current cash balance. The values are entered into the corresponding cells later when you have the actual income and expenses numbers.

You should choose the same cells as defined in this chapter to set up your cashbook.

What is still missing, which is vital for a 'proper' cashbook? The company name! Enter it in cell 'B4'.

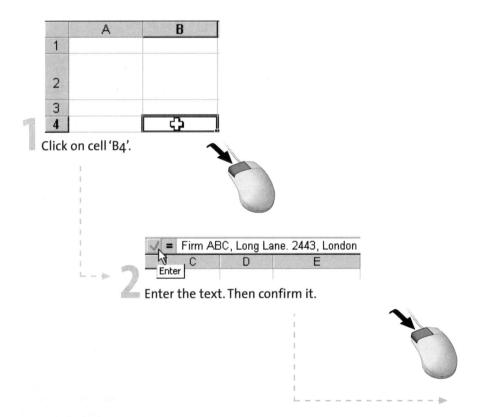

Click on cell 'B4'.

Enter the text. Then confirm it.

	A	B	C	D	E	F
1						
2			Cashbook			
3						
4		Firm ABC, Long Lane. 2443, London				
5						
6		Balance C/O				Earnings
7		Final cash balance				Expenses

3 Write the remaining data into the appropriate cells.

B6: 'Balance c/o'

B7: 'Final cash balance'

F6: 'Earnings'

F7: 'Expenses'

Highlighting cells with borders

As already mentioned, you are going to calculate the values later. The amounts will then be displayed next to the corresponding text.

To highlight the cells even more, you can create a **border** around them. In this case, this is done with lines on the side of the cells.

Balance C/O		Earnings	
Final cash balance		Expenses	

You must click on the cell which you want to surround with a border.

Click on the **arrow** to the right of the *Borders* button. A sub-menu with various types of borders is displayed.

You can see that some lines in the images are shown as black. These are for specifying the border.

You notice a black line to the left or right, at the top or bottom, partly mixed, something of everything. With this image you can put a border around more than two cells. Thus all marked cells will be bordered.

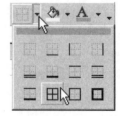

TIP

If you want to put a border around two or more cells, they must first be marked.

In the example cashbook, you will highlight the cells *Balance c/o* and *Final cash balance* in this way.

CAUTION

You cannot delete borders with the [Del] key. You must instead reactivate the Borders menu and choose 'No Border'.

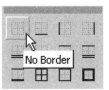

1 Select the two cells 'D6' and 'D7'.

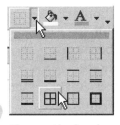

2 Choose the border as shown.

TIP

In Excel the **last used** BORDER is always shown. If you want to apply it again, you do not need to activate the drop-down list, but it is enough to click on the button. This border is shown until you choose a different one.

263

1 Select the cells 'G6' and 'G7'

2 Click on the *Border* button.

The heading for your 'cashbook' is now complete. Next, let us deal with the cells for income and expenses.

Putting a border around a row

To separate the individual areas, you will use another type of border. The expression 'border' might be a bit confusing, because you are going to

Firm ABC, Long Lane. 2443, London	
Balance C/O	
Final cash balance	

choose a display where the **bottom line** of the cell is double underlined.

1 Place the mouse pointer on the ninth row.

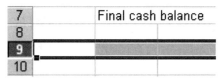

2 Click once: the whole row has been selected.

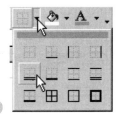

3 Select the border as shown.

Balance C/O	
Final cash balance	

4 Remove the selection with a click anywhere on the worksheet.

265

Preparing cells for future entries

The next steps prepare the cells for the cashbook form. Thus, later you only need to enter the income and expenses amounts.

Changing the column width

Now to the bottom part of the cashbook! You choose the text:

'Serial No., Text, Income, Expenses, Cash'.

To make working with the cells easier, adjust the individual **column widths** in advance. Under 'Serial No.' only a number is entered. The column does not have to be quite as big. Therefore, you can reduce it. In contrast, the column 'Text' will surely require more space. Enlarge it.

Move the mouse pointer between two columns – to be more precise: to the top between two column names. The mouse pointer changes its shape. As soon as it has this appearance you can change the column width, pressing the mouse button.

	A	B	C	D	E	F	G
3							
4		Firm ABC, Long Lane. 2443, London					
5							
6		Balance C/O				Earnings	
7		Final cash balance				Expenses	
8							
9							
10							
11		Serial No.	Text	Income	Expenses	Cash	

1 Write the following text into the cells:
B11: 'Serial No.'

C11: 'Text'

D11: 'Income'

E11: 'Expenses'

F11: 'Cash'

2 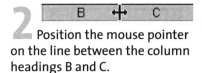 Position the mouse pointer on the line between the column headings B and C.

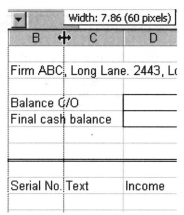

3 Reduce the width of column B to the same size as the image 'Width: 5.00'.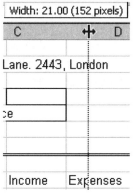

4 Place the mouse pointer between columns C and D.

You cannot select the whole row this time, as only individual cells are going to be bordered.

5 Enlarge the column C accordingly to 'Width: 21.00'.

Again, mark the cells and click on the appropriate border.

267

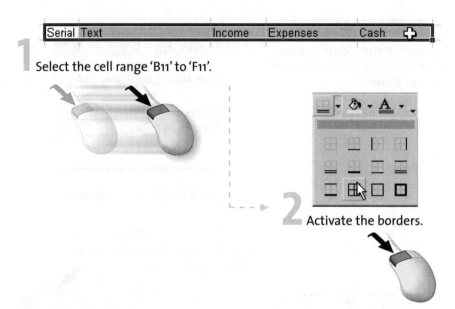

Select the cell range 'B11' to 'F11'.

Activate the borders.

Two borders in one cell

The lower areas are going to be separated by two borders, too. One left border and one right border. Unfortunately, in Excel this combination is not offered as a package!

Now you could select the cells and choose the appropriate borders. But you would not be using this book if you did not want to try a new method. Both methods take the same amount of time and achieve the same goal!

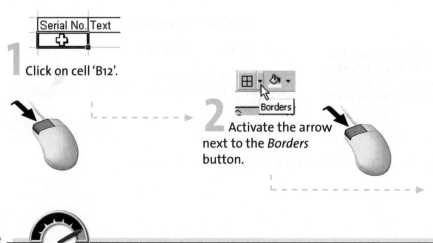

Click on cell 'B12'.

Activate the arrow next to the *Borders* button.

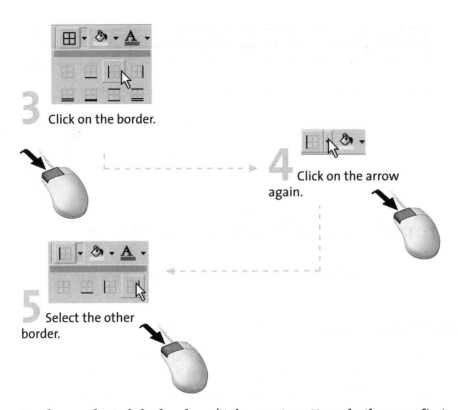

3 Click on the border.

4 Click on the arrow again.

5 Select the other border.

You have selected the borders. (It does not matter whether you first select the left and then the right border or vice versa.)

Copying borders

Move the mouse pointer onto the **fill handle** and, holding down the mouse button, drag into the remaining cells. In this way you can **copy** the existing borders.

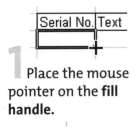

1 Place the mouse pointer on the **fill handle**.

Serial No.	Text	Income	Expenses	Cash

2 Drag to the right up to cell 'F12'. Then release the mouse button.

Formatting cells for future numbers

Patience! Do not yet enter text and numbers. You will see why later on.

Pounds and pence

If you entered numbers, they would look pretty 'bare'. Their value is meaningless without a reference to what they represent. Eggs, pears, apples, or what? In an English cashbook you need to specify **pound sterling.**

To format a cell, you must click on it. If you want to format two or more cells you need to select the corresponding cell range.

The income and the expenses are not always 'whole numbers'. There may be pence, too. Thus, the cell should be formatted with two **decimal places.**

When you click on a cell and press the right mouse button, a **Context menu** is displayed. (You can also select the FORMAT/CELLS menu command. It is exactly the same.)

The name **Context menu** refers to the fact that the composition of the individual menu items depends on what you are doing when you press the right mouse button. Each command can also be executed via the Menu bar.

You can open the correct **Format Cells** dialog box with the [Ctrl] + 1 KEYBOARD SHORTCUT.

You first press the [Ctrl] key, hold it down, and then type 1 on the numerical keypad.

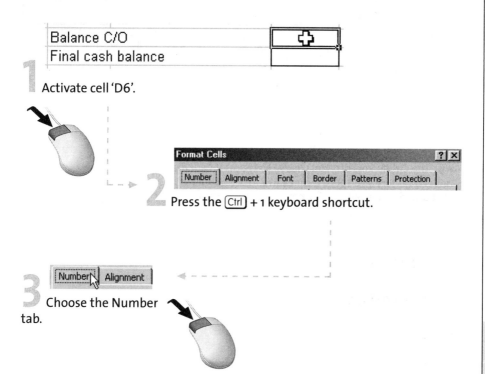

Balance C/O

Final cash balance

1 Activate cell 'D6'.

Format Cells   ? X

| Number | Alignment | Font | Border | Patterns | Protection |

2 Press the [Ctrl] + 1 keyboard shortcut.

| Number | Alignment |

3 Choose the Number tab.

On the *Number* tab you define the **cell format**. Under *Category* you can see the individual areas. There you can find 'Currency'. Under *Symbol*, both pound sterling and euro are listed.

271

With the Format Cells dialog box you can also format cells with other **currencies**. For example, when you buy tulips from Amsterdam, you can format the cells 'hfl', so the value will appear as Dutch guilders.

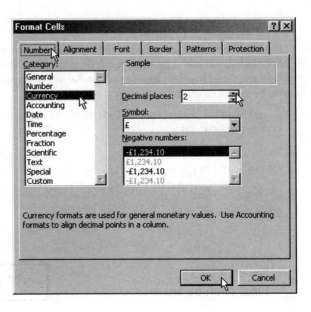

Remember to specify the **decimal places**. For pence or cents you will need '2'. You can close the Format Cells dialog box with the OK button.

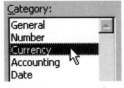

1 Under *Category* select 'Currency'.

2 Specify the currency format '£' and the two decimal places. (Usually they are specified automatically.)

3 Confirm with *OK*.

Transferring existing formats

Do not enter any numbers yet! If you were to enter numbers, Excel would know: this cell contains the currency format '£' with two decimals.

Balance C/O	£200.00
Final cash balance	

However, this is not the only cell for which you have to specify a format. The cell below 'Income' is also bare.

Serial No	Text	Income	Expenses	Cash
1	Cheque	£200.00		

The cells for 'expenses' and 'cash' also have to be formatted. You do not have to repeat the same procedure. Once is more than enough. Life is EASY.

With the **Format Painter** button you can transfer the currency format (including the two decimals) to other cells. With one mouse-click you can **transfer** the **format** only once. Since you need to apply it to several cells, **double-click** on the brush symbol. In this way you can apply the format any number of times.

Format Transfer button	*EFFECT*
Single click	You can transfer the existing format once.
Double click	You **can transfer the existing format** any number of times.

273

A brush has appeared at the mouse pointer. The function has been activated.

You can only transfer existing formats, when the brush is displayed at the mouse pointer.

The function remains activated until you click on the button again or press the Esc key. Then the brush disappears.

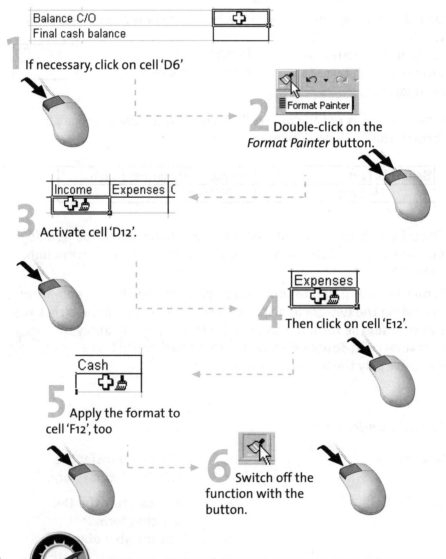

Balance C/O
Final cash balance

1 If necessary, click on cell 'D6'

Format Painter

2 Double-click on the *Format Painter* button.

Income | Expenses | C

3 Activate cell 'D12'.

Expenses

4 Then click on cell 'E12'.

Cash

5 Apply the format to cell 'F12', too

6 Switch off the function with the button.

Different font colours

Expenses make you see 'red. So why not display the values for expenses in red? However, there are also other **colours** to choose from. When you click on the arrow next to the *Font Color* button, a range of various colours is displayed in a sub-menu. For instance, you could choose 'red' for your mail. With a mouse-click on the appropriate colour – red, in this case – you can format the active cell.

1 Click on cell 'E12'.

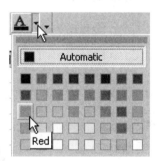

2 Activate the arrow next to the *Font Color* button.

3 Choose the colour 'Red'.

275

If ... then ... else ...

If you had entered
the first record, the
cashbook would look
like this. However, you
are not going to enter
anything just yet.
Later!

Balance C/O		£200.00		Income
Final cash balance				Expenses
Serial No	Text	Income	Expenses	Cash
1	Cheque	£200.00		

Placing formulas in cells

You still have to enter the **formulas**. There is only one: a formula to
calculate the current **cash balance**. In the first case the 'Balance c/o'
and the 'Income' have to be added. However, as you do not know
whether the record is income or an expense, it may also be that the
cash balance is reduced.

Specify in a formula:

If it is income, then add, and if it is expenses, then subtract.

If ...	Calculation
Income	Cash balance + Income
Expenses	Cash balance + Expenses

To enter a formula, start the **Function Wizard.**

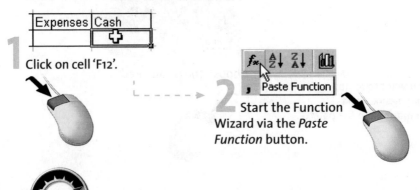

1 Click on cell 'F12'.

2 Start the Function
Wizard via the *Paste
Function* button.

You need the **IF** function. If you do not know in which category you can find a specific function, activate 'All'. This is where all functions which are available in Excel are listed. If you have already used the function, it is advisable to look under 'Last used'. However, that does not apply to you in this case. Therefore, select the **Logical** category. This is where you will find the **IF** function.

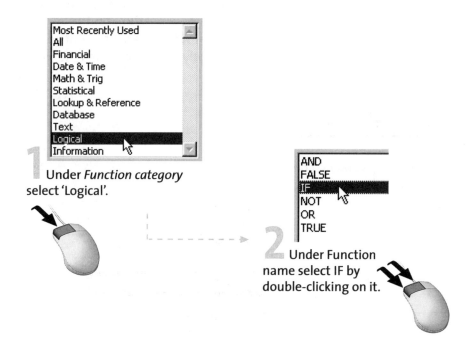

Under *Function category* select 'Logical'.

Under Function name select IF by double-clicking on it.

Moving the entry box

You need to be able to view the cells which are covered by the entry box. Therefore, you are going to move it to a different position in the worksheet.

To move it, simply click on the grey area, and hold down the mouse button. The mouse pointer changes into an **arrow.**

277

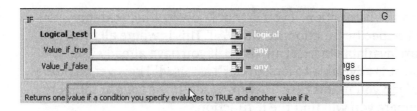

IF			G
Logical_test		= logical	
Value_if_true		= any	
Value_if_false		= any	gs
			ses

Returns one value if a condition you specify evaluates to TRUE and another value if it

When moving the box, you will notice a dotted outline, which has the same size as the entry box. Move it into its new position on the worksheet. (When you restart the Function Wizard later, the entry box will appear in its old position. It will only ever remain in a new position until one entry is completed.)

1 Place the mouse pointer on the grey area in the entry box.

Logical_test	
Value_if_true	
Value_if_false	

urns one value if a condition you specify evaluates to TRU
luates to FALSE.
Logical_test is any value or expression that can be ev

Formula result =

	Serial No.	Text

2 Holding down the mouse button, drag ...

| Balance C/O | | | | Earnings | |
| Final cash balance | | | | Expenses | |

| Serial No. | Text | | Income | Expenses | Cash |
| | | | | | =IF() |

IF			
Logical_test			= logical
Value_if_true			= any
Value_if_false			= any

3 ... the entry box exactly under the cells you are going to work with: 'B12' to 'F12'.

If your first attempt is not successful, keep trying until you reach the target area. Of course, you can also type the cell names into the boxes.

If ...

If only! Your computer knows only two cases or state of affairs: Yes or no!

As the program sees it: if it is not a woman, then it is a man. There is no in-between (for the software).

Condition	Condition does not apply
Man	Woman
Hearing	Dumb
Seeing	Blind
Death	Life
On	Off
Income	Outgoings

279

In this example you are trying to phrase a condition. If it is not **income** it must be an **expense**. There is no in-between!

Enter the condition:

'Income > 0'

When you enter a value under *Income*, Excel knows that it is incoming money and has to be added.

If it is not income, Excel knows that it must be an expense.

If ...	Calculation
Income	Cash balance + Income
Not income	Cash balance - Expenses

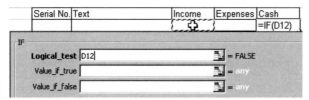

1 If necessary, click on *Logical_test*. Then activate cell 'D12'.

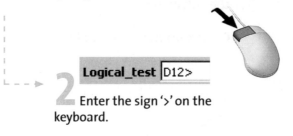

Logical_test D12>

2 Enter the sign '>' on the keyboard.

Logical_test D12>0

3 Type the number '0'.

... Else ...

If it is not income, then it must be an **expense.** The balance c/o is thus reduced by the amount of the expense. Click on *If_false_value* and activate the cells. For the subtraction use the sign '-'.

If ...	Calculation
No income	Cash balance - Expense

> You do not need to enter the '+' sign. If you do not specify an operator, Excel knows that the marked cells need to be added.

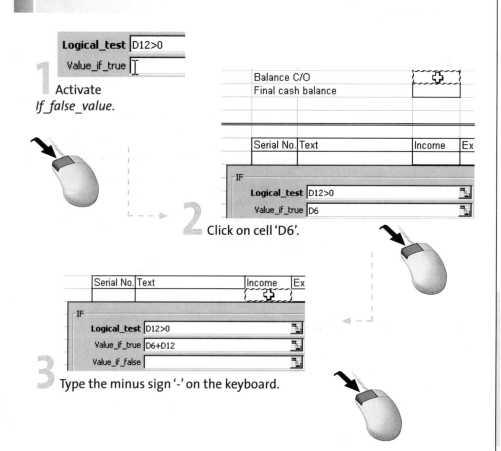

1 Activate *If_false_value*.

2 Click on cell 'D6'.

3 Type the minus sign '-' on the keyboard.

... Else ...

If an entry is not in the Income columns, Excel takes it to be an
Expense. The balance c/o is thus reduced by the expense. Now click
on the *Else_value* and activate the cells. For subtraction, use '-'

Then ...	calculation
No income entry	Cash balance - Expense

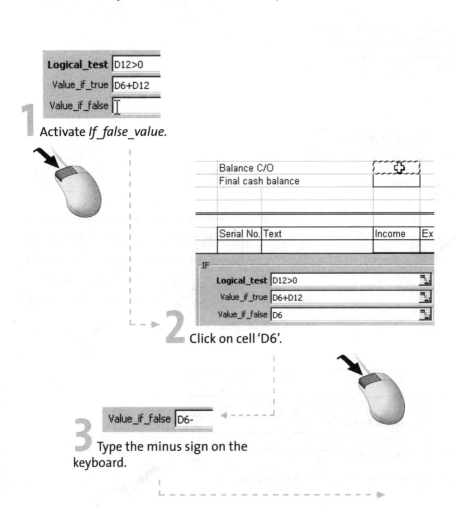

Logical_test D12>0
Value_if_true D6+D12
Value_if_false

1 Activate *If_false_value*.

Balance C/O
Final cash balance

| Serial No. | Text | Income | Ex |

IF
Logical_test D12>0
Value_if_true D6+D12
Value_if_false D6

2 Click on cell 'D6'.

Value_if_false D6-

3 Type the minus sign on the keyboard.

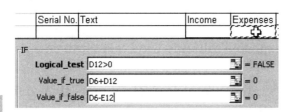

Serial No.	Text	Income	Expenses

IF

Logical_test	D12>0	= FALSE
Value_if_true	D6+D12	= 0
Value_if_false	D6-E12	= 0

4 Click on cell 'E12'.

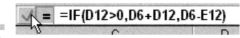

= =IF(D12>0,D6+D12,D6-E12)

5 Complete the formula entry in the Formula bar.

After you have entered the formula, you will notice a balance of '£ 0.00' under *Cash*. This is correct, as you have not yet entered anything.

Cash
0

In the Formula bar, you can see that the cell contains a formula.

WHAT'S THIS?

The **structure** of a **formula** is called the **syntax**.

The semicolon (;) separates the individual instructions.

Syntax

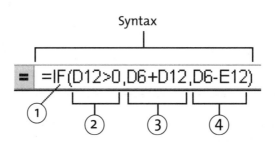

= =IF(D12>0,D6+D12,D6-E12)

① ② ③ ④

283

Expression		Meaning
(IF	①	If ...
D12>0	②	.... the income (cell D12) is more than zero; then ...
D6 + D12	③	... add the balance c/o (cell D6) and the income (cell D12);
D6 - E12)	④	... subtract the expenses (cell E12) from the balance c/o

If you recorded a business transaction, Excel would calculate it correctly. In this case, you have a balance c/o of £ 200 and an **income** of £ 200 (200 + 200 = 400).

Acme co., 12 Long Lane, London SE5 2RJ

Balance C/O	£200.00		Income
Final cash balance			Expenses

Serial No	Text	Income	Expenses	Cash
1	Cheque	£200.00		£400.00

You will also get the correct results for an **expense**. Here you have a balance c/o of £ 200 and an expense of £ 100 (200 - 100 = 100). If your cashbook looks like this, your accounts will always balance.

Balance C/O	£200.00		Income
Final cash balance			Expenses

Serial No	Text	Income	Expenses	Cash
1	Cheque		£100.00	£100.00

However, do not enter any values just yet. You are going to need the blank form later on in this chapter.

The serial number

There is one entry you can make now. Enter the number '1' under 'Serial No.'.

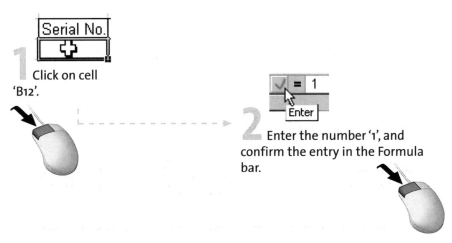

Click on cell 'B12'.

Enter the number '1', and confirm the entry in the Formula bar.

Select the whole row and copy it into the row below with the **fill handle.** You will notice that Excel automatically counts from '1' to '2' under 'Serial No.'.

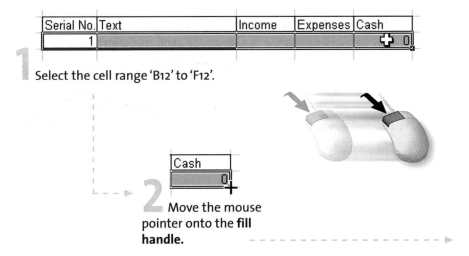

Select the cell range 'B12' to 'F12'.

Move the mouse pointer onto the **fill handle.**

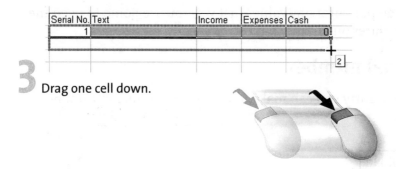

Serial No.	Text	Income	Expenses	Cash
1				0
				2

3 Drag one cell down.

If you want to do without the 'Serial No.' column, it is sufficient to copy the formula in the 'Cash' cell (cell 'F12') downwards.

Modifying the formula

Balance C/O				Earnings
Final cash balance				Expenses

Serial No.	Text	Income	Expenses	Cash
1				0
2				0

However, there is a (logical) error in the formula. From the second row onwards the cash balance is not calculated as before. The first row is actually an exception, as it is the only one which refers to the balance c/o.

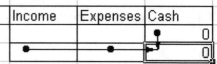

Income	Expenses	Cash
		0
		0

From the second row onwards the current cash balance is always derived from the preceding cash balance.

The formula has to be modified accordingly. You can edit it by clicking on the cell.

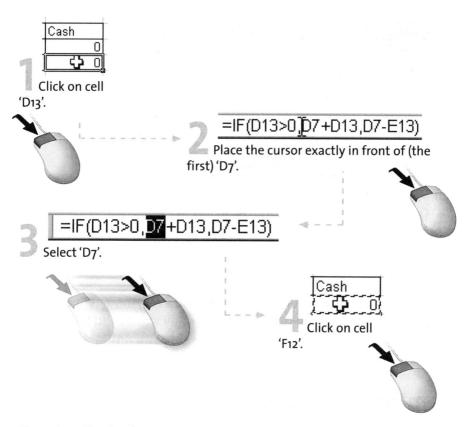

1 Click on cell 'D13'.

2 Place the cursor exactly in front of (the first) 'D7'.

=IF(D13>0,D7+D13,D7-E13)

3 Select 'D7'.

=IF(D13>0,D7+D13,D7-E13)

4 Click on cell 'F12'.

There is still a further occurrence of the wrong cell 'D7' in the Formula bar. Enter the correct cell for the formula.

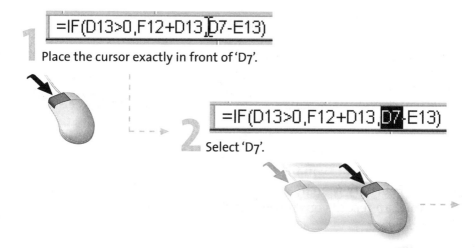

=IF(D13>0,F12+D13,D7-E13)

1 Place the cursor exactly in front of 'D7'.

=IF(D13>0,F12+D13,D7-E13)

2 Select 'D7'.

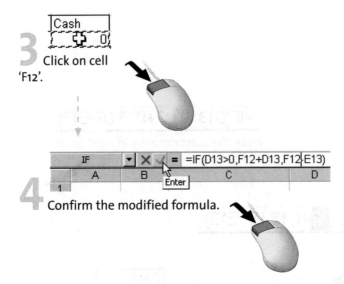

3 Click on cell 'F12'.

IF	▼	X	✓	=	=IF(D13>0,F12+D13,F12-E13)

	A	B	C	D
1				

4 Confirm the modified formula.

From now on you can enter transactions and everything will be calculated correctly. However, do not enter any values yet! We will soon disclose the secret of why we keep asking you not to do it! Have you managed to restrain yourself?

Naming worksheets

It is very likely that you want to use your cashbook for more than just one month. At the bottom you can see the **Sheet tabs** of Excel.

\Sheet1 / Sheet2 / Sheet3 /

Here you can rename the individual worksheets. Thus, you can create one for 'January', one for 'February', and so on.

▶\ **January** / Sheet2 /

In general office practice, this is comparable to a ring binder with the label 'Cash 2000'. Here you file the individual cash sheets under 'January, February, March', and so on. It works just like that in Excel. Thus, you can record your income and your expenses throughout the whole year.

Move the mouse pointer to
the Sheet tabs.

Double-click on
the Sheet tab 'Sheet1'.

The Sheet tab 'Sheet1' is marked black. You only have to type the
name, in this example 'January'.

The Sheet tab has been selected.

Type in the month
'January'.

Confirm the entry with
a mouse-click anywhere on
the worksheet.

289

Copying between worksheets

So far you have only drawn up a blank form for your cashbook. There are good reasons for this! You are going to copy your entries into a new worksheet which you will call 'February'. Thus, you only need to draw up your cashbook once and then only need to copy it for all other months.

Copying from one worksheet to the next is EASY. Position the mouse pointer on the Sheet tab – here 'January'. When you press the left mouse button, a small sheet appears at the mouse pointer. With it you can move the contents of January to the next worksheet. However, that is not what you want to do. You want to copy the worksheet.

When you press the Ctrl key together with the left mouse button, a plus (+) appears in the little sheet next to the mouse pointer.
Now you can **copy**. Drag from one Sheet tab to the next.

1
Move the mouse pointer onto the 'January' Sheet tab.

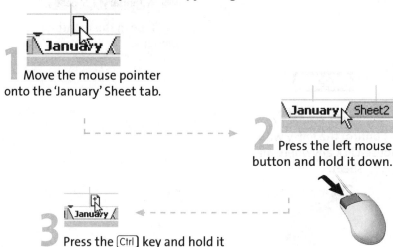

2
Press the left mouse button and hold it down.

3
Press the Ctrl key and hold it down.

4 As both your hands are busy now, drag the mouse button onto the next Sheet tab 'Sheet2'.First release the mouse button and then the Ctrl key!

Excel automatically jumps to the next worksheet to display its contents.

You will notice that a new Sheet tab has been created. It is called 'January (2)'.

Firm ABC, Long Lane. 2443, London					
Balance C/O				Earnings	
Final cash balance				Expenses	
Serial No.	Text		Income	Expenses	Cash
1					0
2					0

▶ ▶❘ \ January \ **January (2)** / Sheet2 / Sheet3 /

As the second worksheet is supposed to be called '**February**', you need to rename it. Proceed in the same way as earlier with the 'January' Sheet tab.

1 Move the mouse pointer to the 'January(2)' Sheet tab.

2 Double-click on it.

291

3 | January (2) |

The name 'January(2)' has been selected.

- - - - - - - - ►

4 | January | **February** | Sheet2 | Sheet3 |

Type in the month 'February'. Confirm the entry with a mouse-click anywhere on the worksheet.

In this way you can create any month you want.

Of course, you can also create different filing options, apart from month by month, such as:

➜ Data for customers, suppliers, private addresses, ...

➜ Days: Monday, Tuesday, ...

➜ Years: 2000, 2001, 2002, ...

Calculating between worksheets

There is one more thing you have to specify on the 'February' worksheet. The **balance c/o** of 'February' derives from the **final cash balance** of 'January'.

Click on the **balance c/o** in February and enter the **equal sign** for a **formula.**

| Balance C/O | ✚ |
| Final cash balance | |

1 In 'February' click – as displayed here – on cell 'D6'.

2 Enter the equal sign for a formula entry.

With a mouse-click on the **Sheet tab,** choose January. Here you only have to click on the final cash balance.

\ January	**February**

1 Click at the bottom on the 'January' Sheet tab.

Balance C/O	
Final cash balance	

2 Click on the 'not yet existing' final cash balance in cell 'D7'.

= =January!D7

3 Confirm the entry.

293

You will notice the value
'£0.00' under balance c/o.
As you have not yet entered

Balance C/O	0
Final cash balance	

any values under January, this is absolutely correct.

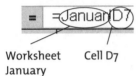

Worksheet
January

Cell D7

When you click on the cell, you can see the
following formula in the Formula bar. The
expression 'January!' means that the formula
refers to the 'January' **worksheet**. This is the
specification of the **cell** (in this case 'D7').

Entering income or expenses

You can now finally make your entries! The advantage of our way of
proceeding is obvious: **now you only need to enter the transactions**.
Everything else is taken care of by the cashbook or the prepared cells.

Watch how the individual cells of the cashbook are automatically
filled while you are entering the values.

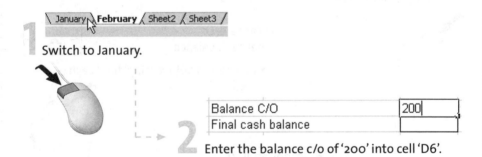

1 | January | **February** | Sheet2 | Sheet3 |

Switch to January.

Balance C/O	200
Final cash balance	

2 Enter the balance c/o of '200' into cell 'D6'.

Firm ABC, Long Lane. 2443, London	
Balance C/O	£ 200.00
Final cash balance	

3 Confirm with the ⏎-key.

4

Serial No.	Text	Income	Expenses	Cash
1	Bank	£ 200.00		£ 400.00

Enter the first transaction.

Surely you want to record more than one business transaction!

1

Serial No.	Text	Income	Expenses	Cash
1	Bank	£ 200.00		£ 400.00
2				£ 400.⟐

Select the second cell.

Cash
£ 400.00
£ 400.00

2 Move the mouse pointer onto the **fill handle**.

3

Serial No.	Text	Income	Expenses	Cash
1	Bank	£ 200.00		£ 400.00
2				£ 400.00
				3

Drag the cells downwards.

4

Serial No.	Text	Income	Expenses	Cash
1	Bank	£ 200.00		£ 400.00
2	Water Rates		£ 80.00	£ 320.00
3				£ 320.00

Enter the second transaction.

Excel automatically numbers entries under '**Serial No.**'. Furthermore, the **formula** for the current cash balance is automatically **copied** into the next row.

295

Carry on in the same way. You can also enter several transactions at once. Thus, day after day, week after week goes by, and the month is soon over.

Serial No.	Text	Income	Expenses	Cash
1	Bank	£ 200.00		£ 400.00
2	Water Rates		£ 80.00	£ 320.00
3				£ 320.0

1 Select the row.

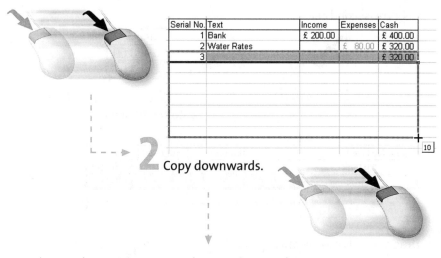

Serial No.	Text	Income	Expenses	Cash
1	Bank	£ 200.00		£ 400.00
2	Water Rates		£ 80.00	£ 320.00
3				£ 320.00

10

2 Copy downwards.

Serial No.	Text	Income	Expenses	Cash
1	Bank	£ 200.00		£ 400.00
2	Water Rates		£ 80.00	£ 320.00
3	Telephone		£ 200.00	£ 120.00
4	Excel EASY		£ 29.95	£ 90.05
5	Job Pay	£ 115.00		£ 205.05
6	Private		£ 200.00	£ 5.05
7	Bank	£ 400.00		£ 405.05
8	Job Pay	£ 575.00		£ 980.05
9	Word EASY		£ 29.95	£ 950.10
10				£ 950.10

3 Enter the income or the expenses.

9	Word EASY		£ 29.95	£ 950.10
10	Final Balance			£ 950.10

4 The month is over! Write 'Final balance' into cell C21.

Time flies. How soon a month is over.

Now you only have to set up the cells for the 'cashbook heading':

➥ Final balance

➥ Total Income

➥ Total Expenses

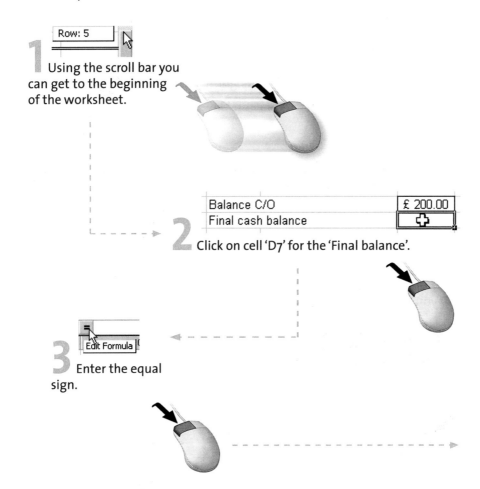

1 Using the scroll bar you can get to the beginning of the worksheet.

Row: 5

| Balance C/O | £ 200.00 |
| Final cash balance | ✚ |

2 Click on cell 'D7' for the 'Final balance'.

Edit Formula

3 Enter the equal sign.

| Formula result = 950.1 | | | OK | Cancel | |

Cashbook

Firm ABC, Long Lane. 2443, London

| Balance C/O | £ 200.00 | Earnings |
| Final cash balance | =F21 | Expenses |

Serial No.	Text	Income	Expenses	Cash
1	Bank	£ 200.00		£ 400.00
2	Water Rates		£ 60.00	£ 320.00
3	Telephone		£ 200.00	£ 120.00
4	Excel EASY		£ 29.95	£ 90.05
5	Job Pay	£ 115.00		£ 205.05
6	Private		£ 200.00	£ 5.05
7	Bank	£ 400.00		£ 405.05
8	Job Pay	£ 575.00		£ 980.05
9	Word EASY		£ 29.95	£ 950.10
10	Final Balance			£ 950.10

4 Click on the cell which contains the final balance (in this example: 'F21'). If necessary, use the right-hand scroll bar.

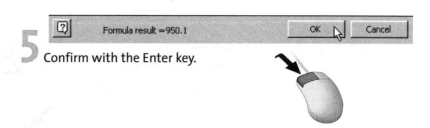

| Formula result = 950.1 | | OK | Cancel |

5 Confirm with the Enter key.

Now you have to establish the **income** TOTAL.

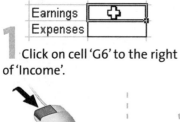

| Earnings | |
| Expenses | |

1 Click on cell 'G6' to the right of 'Income'.

2 Click on the *AutoSum* button.

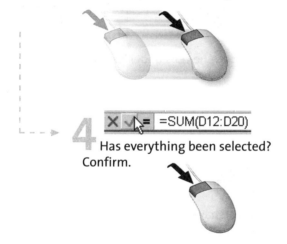

| IF | ▼ | ✕ | ✓ | = | =SUM(D12:D20) |

Cashbook

Firm ABC, Long Lane. 2443, London

Balance C/O	£ 200.00		Earnings	=SUM(D12:D20)
Final cash balance	£ 950.10		Expenses	

Serial No.	Text	Income	Expenses	Cash
1	Bank	£ 200.00		£ 400.00
2	Water Rates		£ 80.00	£ 320.00
3	Telephone		£ 200.00	£ 120.00
4	Excel EASY		£ 29.95	£ 90.05
5	Job Pay	£ 115.00		£ 205.05
6	Private		£ 200.00	£ 5.05
7	Bank	£ 400.00		£ 405.05
8	Job Pay	£ 575.00		£ 980.05
9	Word EASY		£ 29.95	£ 950.10
10	Final Balance			£ 950.10

3 Select the cells under 'Income', that is cell range 'D12' to 'D20'.

| ✕ | ✓ | = | =SUM(D12:D20) |

4 Has everything been selected? Confirm.

Carry out the same procedure for your **expenses**: activate the cell, enter *AutoSum*, and select the appropriate cells.

| Earnings | £ 1,290.00 |
| Expenses | |

1 Click on cell 'G7' for the 'Expenses'.

2 Click on the *AutoSum* button.

Balance C/O	£ 200.00		Earnings	£1,290.00
Final cash balance	£ 950.10		Expenses	=SUM(E12:E20)

Serial No.	Text	Income	Expenses	Cash
1	Bank	£ 200.00		£ 400.00
2	Water Rates		£ 80.00	£ 320.00
3	Telephone		£ 200.00	£ 120.00
4	Excel EASY		£ 29.95	£ 90.05
5	Job Pay	£ 115.00		£ 205.05
6	Private		£ 200.00	£ 5.05
7	Bank	£ 400.00		£ 405.05
8	Job Pay	£ 575.00		£ 980.05
9	Word EASY		£ 29	£ 950.10
10	Final Balance			9R x 1C

3 Select all the cells under 'Expenses', that is cell range 'E12' to 'E20'.

| ✓ = | =SUM(E12:E20) |
| Enter | C |

4 Confirm as soon as you have selected all cells containing expenses.

You might not believe it, but the cashbook is finished! 'January' has been dealt with and is filed. You are ready for 'February'.

Balance C/O	£ 200.00		Earnings	£ 1,290.00
Final cash balance	£ 950.10		Expenses	£ 539.90

Serial No.	Text	Income	Expenses	Cash
1	Bank	£ 200.00		£ 400.00
2	Water Rates		£ 80.00	£ 320.00
3	Telephone		£ 200.00	£ 120.00
4	Excel EASY		£ 29.95	£ 90.05
5	Job Pay	£ 115.00		£ 205.05
6	Private		£ 200.00	£ 5.05
7	Bank	£ 400.00		£ 405.05
8	Job Pay	£ 575.00		£ 980.05
9	Word EASY		£ 29.95	£ 950.10
10	Final Balance			£ 950.10

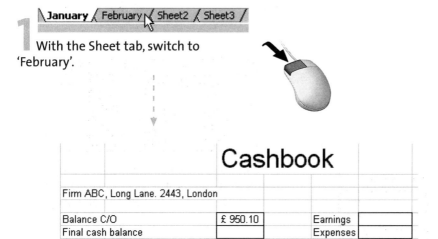

1 With the Sheet tab, switch to 'February'.

Cashbook

Firm ABC, Long Lane. 2443, London				
Balance C/O	£ 950.10		Earnings	
Final cash balance			Expenses	

Under 'Balance c/o' you will notice an amount in '£'. It is the final balance for 'January'.

Well, let's get started with February. Have fun! But remember March is going to be with us sooner or later.

Practise, practise and practise again!

Try to carry out all the steps in the following exercise independently.

Share Profits

Name	No	Buy	Sell	Plus/Minus	Profit/Loss
British Telecom	100	3950	4202		
Air-Hansa	200	2990	3120		
VD	300	23890	24980		
Feba	10	580	460		
German Peanutsbank	100	7890	8600		

1 Create the table for this example.

No	Buy	Sell	Plus/Min
100	3950	4202	=D4-C4
200	2990	3120	
300	23890	24980	
10	580	460	
100	7890	8600	

2 Carry out the calculation within the column 'Plus/Minus'. The sales price ('D4') minus the purchase price ('C4') yield the plus/minus.

Plus/Minus
252
130
1090
-120
710

3 Copy the calculation into the appropriate cells.

Plus/Minus	Pro
252	
130	
1090	
-120	
710	
=SUM(E4:E8	5R

4 Find the total of the column 'Plus/Minus'.

If you have made a profit, the column 'Profit/Loss' should say 'Profit', otherwise 'Loss'.

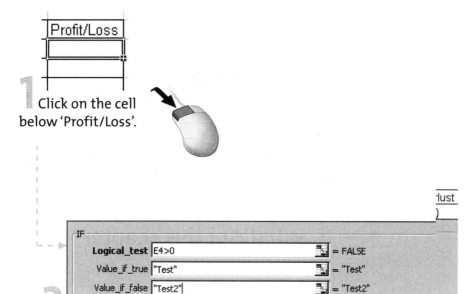

1 Click on the cell below 'Profit/Loss'.

2 Start the **Function Wizard** and choose the **function IF**. Specify the **condition.**

(You do not have to insert the speech marks. Excel automatically inserts them.)

Plus/Minus	Profit/Loss
252	Profit
130	Profit
1090	Profit
-120	Loss
710	Profit
2062	Profit

3 Copy the function into the remaining cells.

Indices for overviews

What's in this chapter?

No more notes on slips of paper! Do you scribble down phone numbers, and the birthdays of family members and friends on slips of paper? What was the address of Mr ABC from XYZ? Never again! With Excel you can create clearly arranged address lists and sort them from A to Z. In this chapter you will do a lot of filtering: AutoFilter, Custom AutoFilter and Advanced Filter. Too much? Have a cup of filter coffee!

Name	First Name	Street	Post Code	City
Adam	Peter	New Road	LS2 4FT	Leeds
Bennett	Helen	Clear Road	B31 5HM	Bath
Breen	Steve	Dore Road	S9 4GA	Sheffield
Edwards	William	Ottley Road	B7 7XY	Bath
Fox	Anne	New Street	EH0 3XY	Edinburgh
Kemp	Mark	Briarfield Avenue	S12 3LA	Sheffield
Moore	Fred	Little Road	GH5 3QS	Gabham
Moore	Tina	Little Road	GH5 3QS	Gabham
Smith	Carle	York Road	LS0 1XX	Leeds
Smith	John	Long Lane	S2 5FT	Sheffield

You already know about:

You are going to learn about:

Sorting lists

You can create indices to record addresses, articles, and so on. Excel assists you in the management of such lists.

You are going to create an address log, to which you can add if you so wish, for example 'birthday, phone number'. To organise it more clearly, you are going to sort the list in alphabetical order.

However, with these two buttons you can only sort the **first column.** In our list this is the column 'Name'.

As it may certainly happen that two people have the same family name, you also have to sort by first names (like in a telephone directory).

Under the DATA/SORT menu option you can define the **criteria.** Here you can sort first by 'Name', and then by 'First Name'. You can make a total of three choices.

Sort by	Example
Name	Adam, Peter, Leeds
	Adam, Hugh, York
	Adam, Hugh, London
	Bennett, Helen, Bath
First Name	Adam, Hugh, York
	Adam, Hugh, London
	Adam, Peter, Leeds
City	Adam, Hugh, Leeds
	Adam, Hugh, York

Please note whether the option 'Headings' is activated when sorting. The lists should contain a heading, otherwise Excel includes it in the sorting process.

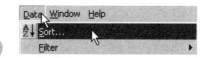

My list has

◉ Header row   ○ No header row

	A	B	C	D	E	F	G
1							
2							
3		**Name**	**First Name**	**Street**		**Post Code**	**City**
4		Smith	John	Long Lane		S2 5FT	Sheffield
5		Adam	Peter	New Road		LS2 4FT	Leeds
6		Bennett	Helen	Clear Road		B31 5HM	Bath
7		Kemp	Mark	Briarfield Avenue		S12 3LA	Sheffield
8		Breen	Steve	Dore Road		S9 4GA	Sheffield
9		Moore	Fred	Little Road		GH5 3QS	Gabham
10		Moore	Tina	Little Road		GH5 3QS	Gabham
11		Smith	Carle	York Road		LS0 1XX	Leeds
12		Edwards	William	Ottley Road		B7 7XY	Bath
13		Fox	Anne	New Street		EH0 3XY	Edinburgh
14							

1 First enter the list.

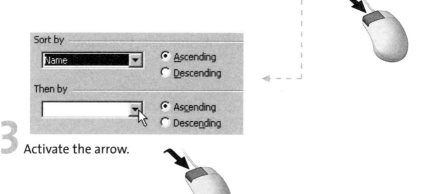

Data Window Help
A↓ Sort...
   Filter

2 Click on a cell within the table. Activate the DATA/SORT menu option.

Sort by

[Name ▼]   ◉ Ascending
            ○ Descending

Then by

[▼]   ◉ Ascending
        ○ Descending

3 Activate the arrow.

4 Select 'First Name'.

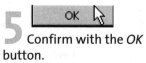

5 Confirm with the *OK* button.

Name	First Name	Street	Post Code	City
Adam	Peter	New Road	LS2 4FT	Leeds
Bennett	Helen	Clear Road	B31 5HM	Bath
Breen	Steve	Dore Road	S9 4GA	Sheffield
Edwards	William	Ottley Road	B7 7XY	Bath
Fox	Anne	New Street	EH0 3XY	Edinburgh
Kemp	Mark	Briarfield Avenue	S12 3LA	Sheffield
Moore	Fred	Little Road	GH5 3QS	Gabham
Moore	Tina	Little Road	GH5 3QS	Gabham
Smith	Carle	York Road	LS0 1XX	Leeds
Smith	John	Long Lane	S2 5FT	Sheffield

6 The list has been sorted.

You can move quickly through lists, and select cells using **keyboard shortcuts:**

KEYS	EFFECT
Ctrl + ↑	First cell in a column
Ctrl + ↓	Last cell in a column
Ctrl + ←	First cell in a row
Ctrl + →	Last cell in a row

Keys	Effect
Ctrl + ⇧ + ⬇	Selects a column
Ctrl + ⇧ + →	Selects a row
Ctrl + ⇧ + *	Selects the whole list

Freezing a list

In very extensive lists it is not very practicable to scroll through them from A to Z on your screen. With the Menu option WINDOW/FREEZE PANES the heading remains fixed.

Name	First Name
Adam	Peter
Bennett	Helen

1 Click exactly on this cell (the first of the addresses).

Data   Window   Help

Freeze Panes

2 Select the WINDOW/ FREEZE PANES.

Name	First Name
Adam	Peter
Bennett	Helen

3 You will notice the lines on the screen.

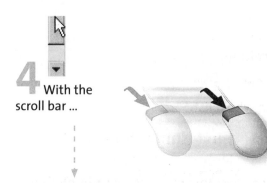

4 With the
scroll bar ...

Name	First Name	Street	Post code	City
Smith	John	Long Lane	S2 5FT	Sheffield

5 ... quickly scroll through the list.

Remove the frozen panes by selecting the **WINDOW/UNFREEZE PANES** menu
option.

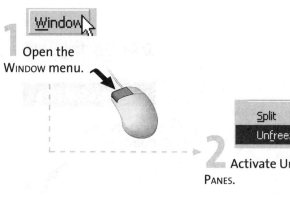

1 Open the
WINDOW menu.

2 Activate UNFREEZE
PANES.

The data form

Excel also has a data form. Click on a cell in the list and choose **Form** in the **Data** menu.

A data record consists of data fields (Name, First name, Street, City, and so on).

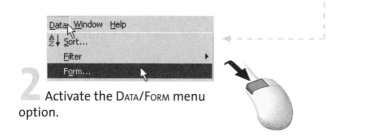

Name	First Name	Street
Adam	Peter	New Road
Bennett	Helen	Clear Road
Breen	Steve	Dore Road

Click on a **cell within the list**.

Activate the **Data/Form** menu option.

From here you can also create and edit addresses.

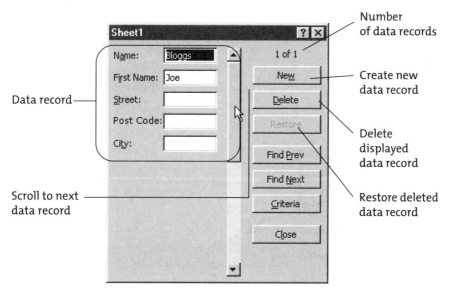

Number of data records

Create new data record

Data record

Delete displayed data record

Scroll to next data record

Restore deleted data record

311

Looking for ...

With the *Criteria* button you can extract individual addresses. When you click on it, you can choose what you want to be displayed. If you only remember the **initial letter** of the name, you can use **wildcards** (*,?). When you enter 'S*', as shown. here, only records of people whose name begins with 'S' are shown.

Wildcard	Entry	Effect
*	S*	All persons whose name begins with 'S' are listed.
?	S??th	Excel lists, for example: Smith, Smyth, South.

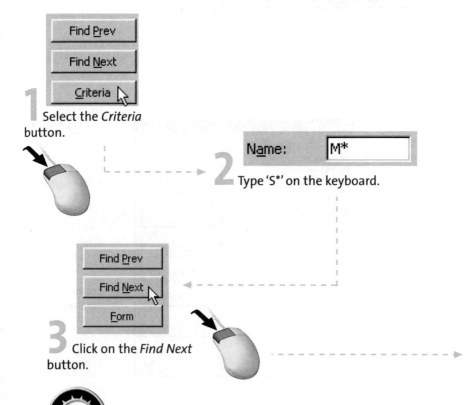

1 Select the *Criteria* button.

Name: M*

2 Type 'S*' on the keyboard.

3 Click on the *Find Next* button.

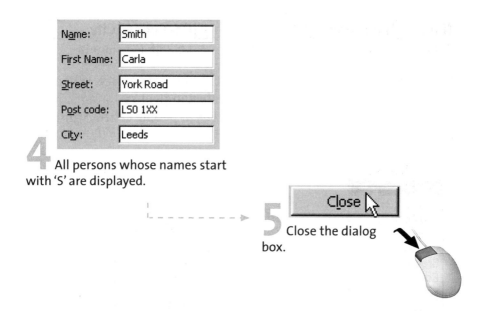

4 All persons whose names start with 'S' are displayed.

5 Close the dialog box.

The AutoFilter

With the 'AutoFilter' you prevent display of specific addresses, by 'filtering' them out. Here you enter **criteria**, too. Again, a **cell within the list** must be activated.

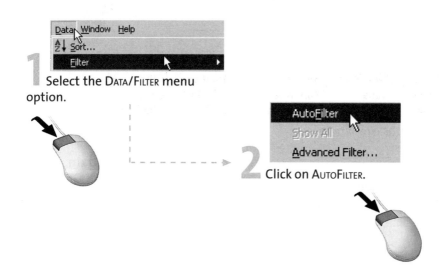

1 Select the DATA/FILTER menu option.

2 Click on AUTOFILTER.

Name ▾	First Nam ▾	Street	▾	Post cod ▾	City	▾
Adam	Peter	New Road		LS2 4FT	Leeds	

After you have activated the *AutoFilter*, this is what you see. When you click on an arrow in a column, you can select individual data records. When you click on 'Smith', all the addresses of people called 'Smith' are displayed.

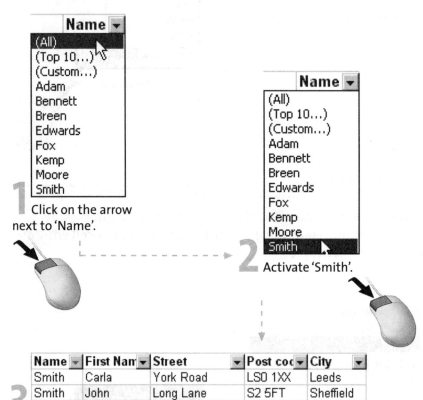

Click on the arrow next to 'Name'.

Activate 'Smith'.

Name ▾	First Nam ▾	Street	▾	Post cod ▾	City	▾
Smith	Carla	York Road		LS0 1XX	Leeds	
Smith	John	Long Lane		S2 5FT	Sheffield	

All 'Smiths' are shown.

If you want to see all records again, activate the arrow and choose '(All)'.

With '(Top 10...)' you can select the top selection: the highest numbers, percent values, and so on.

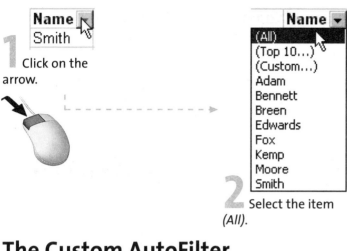

1 Click on the arrow.

2 Select the item *(All)*.

The Custom AutoFilter

You can select a custom AutoFilter for each field in the list. In this example, you wish to extract all cities which are in the postcode area from '50000' to '90000'. Click on the arrow next to the 'Postcode' column and choose *(Custom ...)*. With the *And* option you link the two conditions.

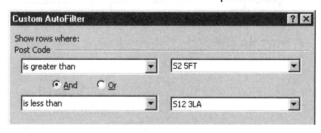

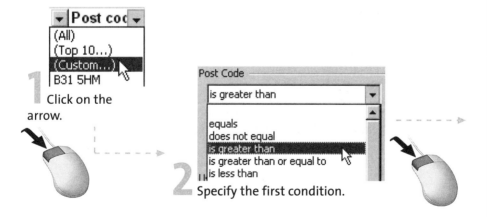

1 Click on the arrow.

2 Specify the first condition.

315

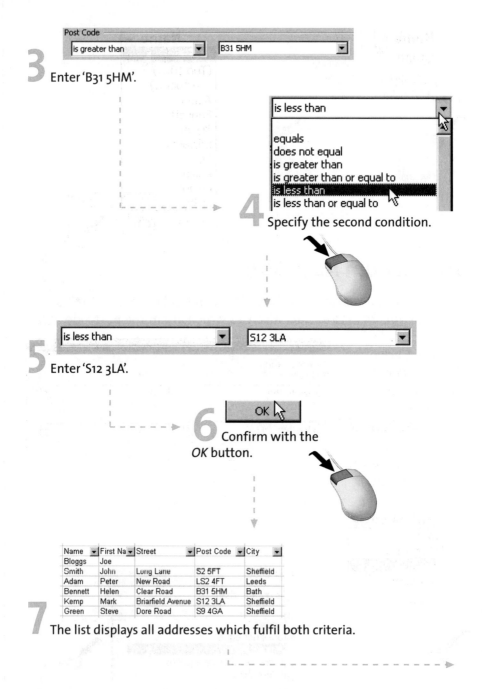

Post Code

| is greater than | ▼ | B31 5HM | ▼ |

3 Enter 'B31 5HM'.

| is less than | ▼ |

| equals |
| does not equal |
| is greater than |
| is greater than or equal to |
| **is less than** |
| is less than or equal to |

4 Specify the second condition.

| is less than | ▼ | S12 3LA | ▼ |

5 Enter 'S12 3LA'.

OK

6 Confirm with the *OK* button.

Name ▼	First Na ▼	Street ▼	Post Code ▼	City ▼
Bloggs	Joe			
Smith	John	Long Lane	S2 5FT	Sheffield
Adam	Peter	New Road	LS2 4FT	Leeds
Bennett	Helen	Clear Road	B31 5HM	Bath
Kemp	Mark	Briarfield Avenue	S12 3LA	Sheffield
Green	Steve	Dore Road	S9 4GA	Sheffield

7 The list displays all addresses which fulfil both criteria.

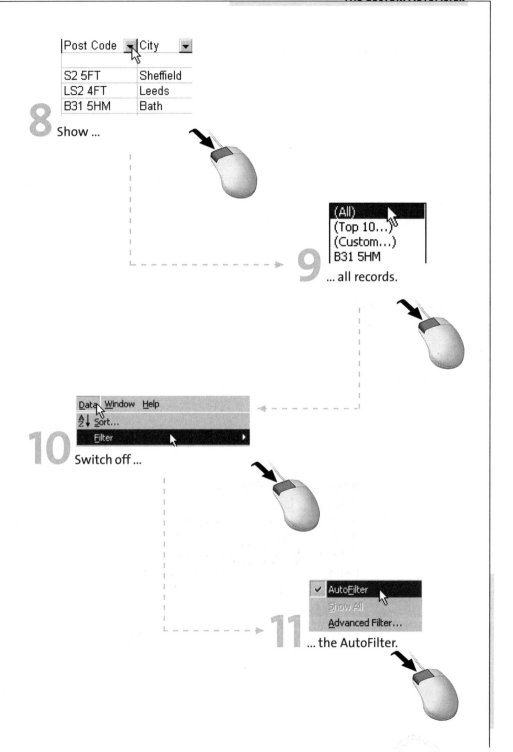

Post Code	City
S2 5FT	Sheffield
LS2 4FT	Leeds
B31 5HM	Bath

8 Show ...

(All)
(Top 10...)
(Custom...)
B31 5HM

9 ... all records.

Data Window Help
A↓ Sort...
    Filter

10 Switch off ...

✓ AutoFilter
   Show All
   Advanced Filter...

11 ... the AutoFilter.

317

The Advanced Filter

Here you have the option to display individual addresses on the sheet. The data records are filtered again. Subsequently you can **copy** the result onto the worksheet.

In this example you are planning to travel to 'Gabham', wherever that place may be. Only people who live there are supposed to be shown. Enter 'City' in one cell, and 'Gabham' in a second cell.

It is important that you activate the corresponding list with a mouse-click. In this way you are telling Excel which data has to be filtered.

Kemp	Mark
Green	Steve
City	
Gabham	

1 Enter the data 'City, Gabham' into the individual cells **under the list.**

Name	First Nam	Street
Bloggs	Joe	
Smith	John	Long Lane
Adam	Peter	New Road
Bennett	Helen	Clear Road
Kemp	Mark	Briarfield Avenue
Green	Steve	Dore Road

2 Click on a cell within the list.

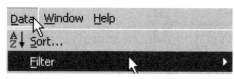

3 Choose the DATA/FILTER menu option.

4 Click on ADVANCED FILTER.

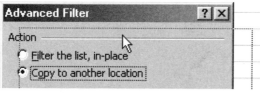

5 In the background Excel selects the list.

6 Specify the option.

319

| List range: | $C$4:$G$10 | |
| Criteria range: | | |

7 Click on *Criteria range*.

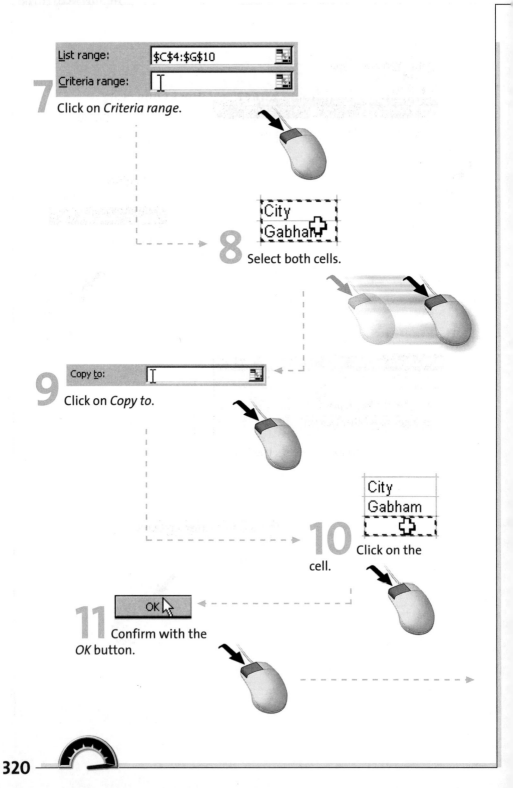

City
Gabha

8 Select both cells.

| Copy to: | | |

9 Click on *Copy to*.

City
Gabham

10 Click on the cell.

OK

11 Confirm with the *OK* button.

City				
Gabham				
Name	**First Name**	**Street**	**Post code**	**City**
Moore	Fred	Little Road	GH5 3QS	Gabham
Moore	Tina	Little Road	GH5 3QS	Gabham

12 The addresses have been extracted.

What's in this chapter?

If you are drowning and you cannot (yet) swim properly, there is only one hope: you need somebody to save you, who will pull you out. But, if nobody is around, what do you do? Do you pray for a lifebelt? Excel offers you lifebelts in the form of numerous help programs. If things do not work out, you can fold your hands and pray for a miracle. Alternatively, you can use the help programs in Excel. There are more of them than you might think!

The Assistant – with a little help from a friend

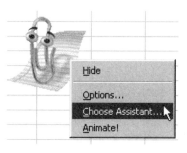

A pleasant, additional feature of Excel is the amusing animations that are available to you. When you click on the *Help* button, the **Assistant** appears on the screen.

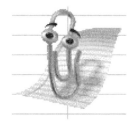

This is 'Clippit', the vivacious paperclip. When you move the mouse pointer on the Assistant and press the **right mouse** button, a Context menu opens.

From here you can get to various points. For example, under OPTIONS you can determine which tips you want the Assistant to display.

Activate the entry ANIMATE! and the Assistant will give a little performance. Activate it with the left mouse button (this is how the pictures in this chapter have been created).

When you click on CHOOSE ASSISTANT, various helpers appear. With the *Forward* and *Back* buttons you can view them one by one.

The choice is yours. If you decide to **change** your **Assistant**, you need to insert the Office 2000 installation CD. Confirm the selected Assistant with *OK*.

Any questions?

Whenever you have a question about Excel, simply click on your Assistant. Enter your query and click on the *Search* button. While you are phrasing your question, your Assistant will make notes. Your query does not have to be in the form of a question. However, it has to be entered in a way your Assistant can understand. Often **keywords** will be enough. In this case 'copying cells' has been entered.

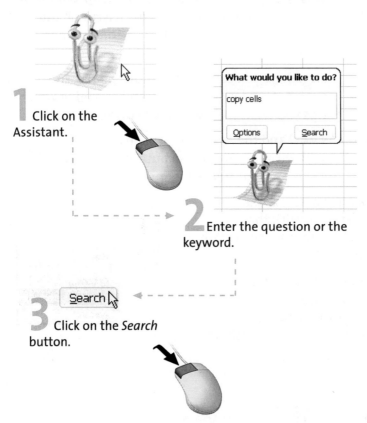

1 Click on the Assistant.

What would you like to do?

copy cells

Options   Search

2 Enter the question or the keyword.

Search

3 Click on the *Search* button.

You will be offered several areas, which may be relevant, as a solution. Pick the most relevant area. Excel offers you information and instructions connected with the topic.

- Copy formats from one cell or range to another
- Copy worksheet cells into a Word document or PowerPoint presentation

1 Select a topic with a mouse-click.

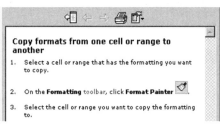

Copy formats from one cell or range to another

1. Select a cell or range that has the formatting you want to copy.

2. On the **Formatting** toolbar, click **Format Painter**.

3. Select the cell or range you want to copy the formatting to.

2 The help topic opens on your screen.

By clicking on the button you can extend the help topic.

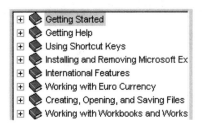

On the *Contents* tab you will find the individual help books. Double-click on a book, and a selection of individual topics is displayed.

When you activate the *Answer Assistant* tab with a mouse-click, you can enter your questions or keywords under *What would you like to do?*

As soon as you click on the *Search* button, Excel presents some suggestions to you.

You can enter keywords, with which you need help, on the *Index* tab. When you enter

What would you like to do?

copy cells

Search

325

your first keyword under *1. Keywords*, you will notice that Excel jumps further and further down the list each time that a new letter is entered. Thus, Excel Help already selects concepts which may be relevant.

Close Excel Help by clicking on the cross on the title bar.

What's this?

A help option everybody should know is 'What's this?'.

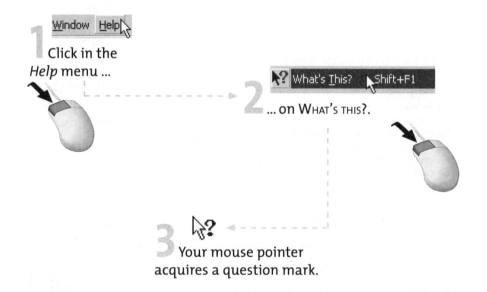

1 Click in the *Help* menu ...

2 ... on WHAT'S THIS?.

3 Your mouse pointer acquires a question mark.

When you, for example, click on a button, you are provided with an extensive **description** instead of the usual ScreenTips. Deactivate *What's this?* with the Esc key.

Even within a **dialog box** you will find additional help. When you click on the question mark at the right end of The title bar a question mark is added to your mouse pointer.

When you now click on any element in the dialog box, you will receive the information you need. Click anywhere on the screen, and the description disappears again.

You can achieve the same effect by **right-clicking** any element within the dialog box. A *What's this?* box is displayed, and you can activate it by clicking on it.

In a dialog box you can also call up the **Assistant**.

The detective

The detective is something of a sniffer dog, as it **'looks for traces'**.

With the TOOLS/AUDITING menu option the 'detective' can be activated. Here you have a choice. With TRACE PRECEDENTS information about cell references for the formula in the cell will be displayed.

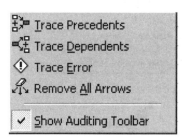

Here the value '48 %' is taken from the two selected cells. The TRACE DEPENDENTS item indicates which cells are dependent from the displayed value. With the SHOW AUDITING TOOLBAR item you can activate the corresponding toolbar on your screen.

CAUTION

You can only use auditing in cells that contain a **formula**.

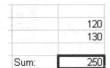

	120
	130
Sum:	250

1 Enter a small calculation. To establish the result click on the AutoSum button. The **cell** must be activated.

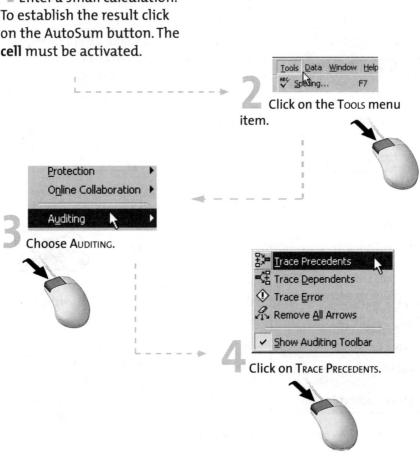

2 Click on the Tools menu item.

3 Choose AUDITING.

4 Click on TRACE PRECEDENTS.

The values to which the formula refers. In this case the corresponding area is framed in blue. This calculation is still easy to understand.

However, in large calculations it can be very informative to know how a value is arrived at.

	120
	130
Sum:	250

Balance C/O	€200.00	Income	£1,290.00
Final cash balance	£950.10	Expenses	£539.90

Serial No	Text	Income	Expenses	Cash
1	Cheque	€200.00		€400.00
2	Stamps		£80.00	€320.00
3	Petty cash		€200.00	€120.00
4	Excel EASY		£29.95	£90.05
5	Cash Payment	€115.00		€205.05
6	Cash (Private)		€200.00	£5.05
7	Cheque	€400.00		€405.05
8	Cash payment	€575.00		€980.05
9	Word EASY		£29.95	€950.10
10	Final cash balance			€950.10

The dots mark the cell that is affected by the formula. The arrows point to the results.

Removing all traces

To remove the traces from your screen, choose *Remove all arrows* in the TOOLS/AUDITING menu option.

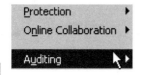

Under TOOLS/AUDITING hide all traces ...

... with REMOVE ALL ARROWS.

329

Hiding/showing formulas

Excel offers further Assistants with the option **Show formulas**. So far you could see them in the Formula bar, when clicking on a cell. Thus, you could only ever see one at a time. Under TOOLS/OPTIONS choose the *View* tab. Under *Window options* activate 'Formulas'. When you click on it a 'tick' appears in the check box. As soon as you confirm with *OK*, you will notice that the numbers are replaced by formulas in your worksheet.

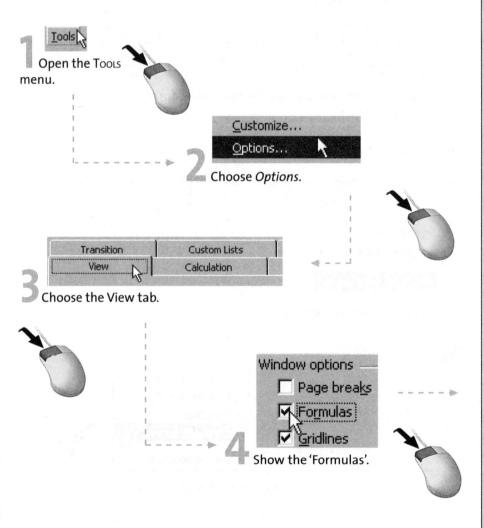

1 Open the TOOLS menu.

2 Choose *Options*.

3 Choose the View tab.

4 Show the 'Formulas'.

5 Confirm with the OK button.

Formulas are now **shown** on your screen. In the figure on the right this does not yet make much sense, as you can check the contents of one cell on the Formula bar, too.

It makes a lot more sense when there are several cells containing formulas. In this

	120
	130
Sum:	=SUM(C6:C8)

case, you can clearly see what has been entered in each cell.

Income	Expenditure	Cash
200		=IF(D12>0,D7+D12,D7D6-E2)
	80	=IF(D13>0,F12+D13,F12-E13)
	200	=IF(D14>0,F13+D14,F13-E14)
	29.95	=IF(D15>0,F14+D15,F14-E15)
115		=IF(D16>0,F15+D16,F15-E16)
	200	=IF(D17>0,F16+D17,F16-E17)
400		=IF(D18>0,F17+D18,F17-E18)
575		=IF(D19>0,F18+D19,F18-E19)
	29.95	=IF(D20>0,F19+D20,F19-E20)

You can hide the **formulas** again by deactivating 'Formulas' on the *View* tab under the TOOLS/OPTIONS menu option.

The mouse pointer and its appearance

The mouse is used to execute various functions. When you move the mouse pointer across the screen you will notice that it frequently changes its appearance. It literally communicates (in sign language) with you, all the time telling you what you can do – commands or entries – at the moment. With a few small exercises you will soon get to know all the options!

The mouse pointer as an arrow

When the pointer looks like this, you can execute commands (such as *Print* or *Save*) on the Excel screen.

(See Chapter 2.)

The mouse pointer as a cross

The **white cross** indicates a position on the worksheet. You can click on a cell and make entries.

(Chapter 2)

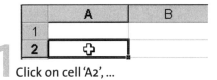

Click on cell 'A2', ...

.... then on cell 'B1'.

The pointer when making entries

When you enter your data – in the cell and/or in the Formula bar – the pointer changes shape again. Only after you have completed your **entries**, does the mouse pointer turn back into a cross.

333

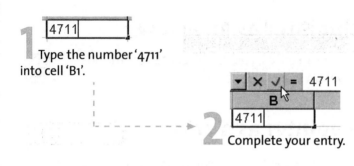

1 Type the number '4711' into cell 'B1'.

2 Complete your entry.

The mouse pointer for filling

You can execute the fill function with the mouse on an Excel worksheet , when this sign appears.

(Chapter 7)

+

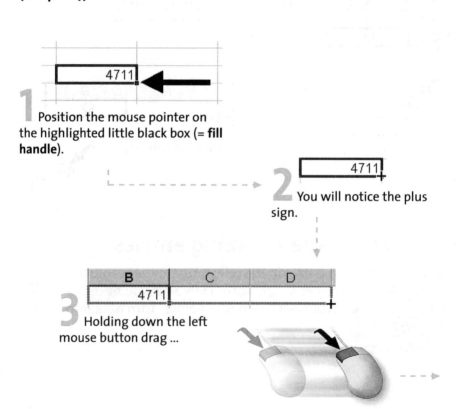

1 Position the mouse pointer on the highlighted little black box (= **fill handle**).

2 You will notice the plus sign.

3 Holding down the left mouse button drag ...

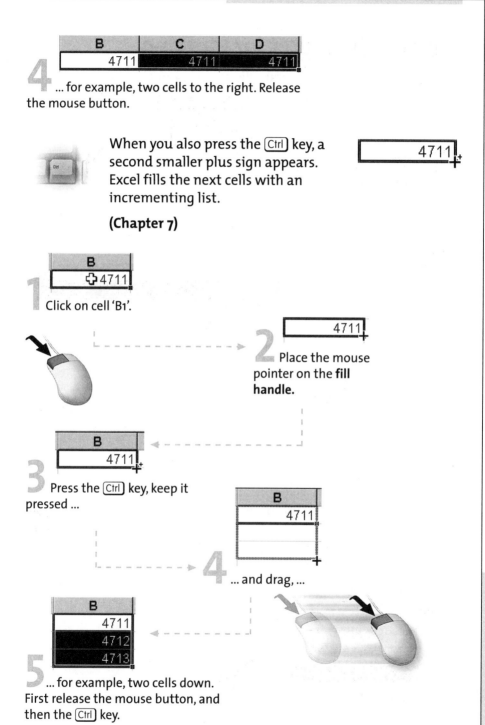

4 ... for example, two cells to the right. Release the mouse button.

When you also press the Ctrl key, a second smaller plus sign appears. Excel fills the next cells with an incrementing list.

(Chapter 7)

1 Click on cell 'B1'.

2 Place the mouse pointer on the **fill handle.**

3 Press the Ctrl key, keep it pressed ...

4 ... and drag, ...

5 ... for example, two cells down. First release the mouse button, and then the Ctrl key.

335

The mouse pointer for marking

When you want to mark several cells at once, you also use the white cross of the mouse pointer.

(Chapter 4)

B	C	D
⊹ 4711	4711	4711
4712		
4713		

Click on cell 'B1'.

B	C	D
4711	4711	✚ 4711
4712		
4713		

Holding down the left mouse button, mark two cells to the right.

The mouse pointer with the ?

When you call up the HELP/WHAT'S THIS? menu item or press the ⇧ + F1 keys, a question mark appears with the mouse pointer. With it you can ask the program the purpose of aspecific button,for example.

(Chapter 15)

Select the HELP/WHAT'S THIS? menu item.

2 With the mouse pointer, click on the button.

You get a corresponding **description**: in this case of the 'Bold' formatting.

With another click of the mouse button, the description disappears from the screen.

Bold (Formatting toolbar)

Makes selected text and numbers **bold.** If the selection is already bold, clicking **B** removes bold formatting.

	A	B	C	D
B1		▼	=	4711
1		4711	4711	4711
2		4712		
3		4713		

1 Press the mouse button once. The description has disappeared from the screen.

2 Click on the button.

B	C	D
4711	**4711**	**4711**
4712	✛	
4713		

3 Click on a cell. The selected cells have been highlighted with bold script.

337

The mouse pointer for adjusting column widths

When you place the mouse pointer between two column names, it changes its shape. By holding down the left mouse button, you can change the **column width** to whatever width you require.

You can do it more quickly with a double click. Excel **automatically adjusts** the column width to accommodate the longest expression (number or word).

(Chapter 4)

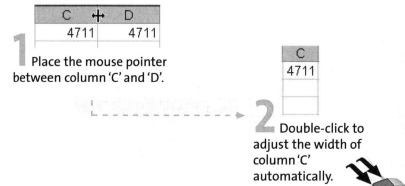

1 Place the mouse pointer between column 'C' and 'D'.

2 Double-click to adjust the width of column 'C' automatically.

The mouse pointer for moving cells

Do you want to move the cells? You do not need to repeat the entry, but you can use the **drag and drop** method.

Drag and drop – YOU CAN MOVE cells ON A **worksheet**.

How to drag and drop

For the successful execution of the drag and drop method the **appearance** of the **mouse pointer** is crucial. It indicates which functions are currently available to you.

On the worksheet, the mouse pointer usually appears as a white cross. With it – as you already know – you click on cells.

Only when the mouse pointer has the shape of an **arrow** on the **worksheet** is it possible to drag and drop.

However, when you position the mouse pointer on the **outline** of

| | 4711 |

the cell highlight, the pointer turns into an **arrow.**

(Chapter 4)

1 | ✛ 4711 |

Click on cell 'D1'.

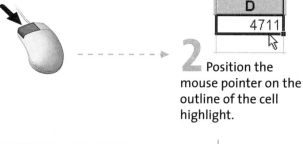

2 Position the mouse pointer on the outline of the cell highlight.

| **D** |
| 4711 |

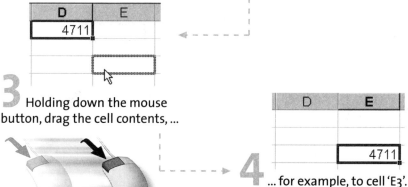

3 Holding down the mouse button, drag the cell contents, ...

| **D** | **E** |
| 4711 | |

4 ... for example, to cell 'E3'. Release the mouse button.

| **D** | **E** |
| | 4711 |

339

The pointer for copying cells

You can also copy cell contents with the drag and drop method .

The procedure is the same as for moving cell contents. Additionally, you have to press the Ctrl key. A small + (Plus) is displayed with the mouse pointer.

(Chapter 7)

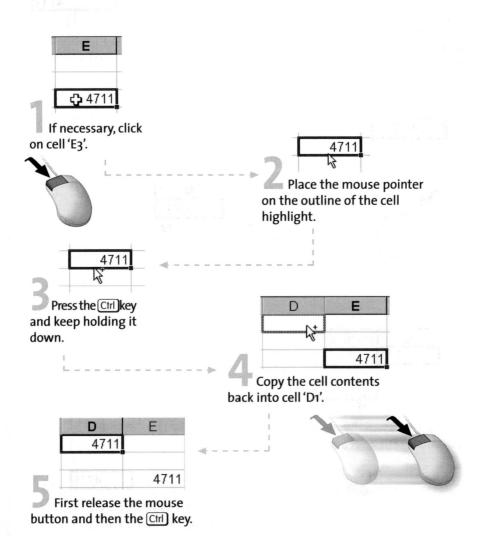

1 If necessary, click on cell 'E3'.

2 Place the mouse pointer on the outline of the cell highlight.

3 Press the Ctrl key and keep holding it down.

4 Copy the cell contents back into cell 'D1'.

5 First release the mouse button and then the Ctrl key.

In black and white: selection made easy

WHAT'S THIS?

You need to select cells if you want to apply the same **formatting** (such as font, font size, bold, and so on) to several cells (= cell range) or if you want to integrate the cells in a calculation (**formula**).

Excel beginners often find selction difficult.

With a few small exercises you will soon master the various selection options.

TIP

To make it easier to understand, hardly any inputting of numbers or text is required here.

Selecting with the mouse

1 Holding down the left mouse button drag into the cells ...

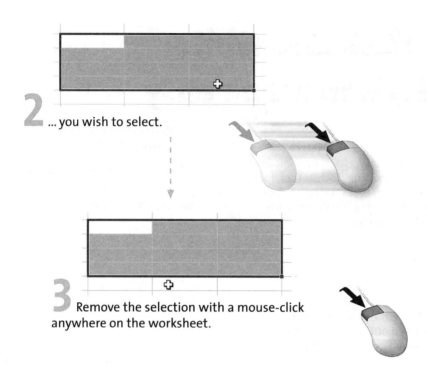

2 ... you wish to select.

3 Remove the selection with a mouse-click anywhere on the worksheet.

Selecting with the keyboard

1 You do not necessarily need the mouse to select cells. You can also select with the keyboard. Activate a cell.

2 Holding down the ⬆ key move the selection with the cursor keys ⬆ ➡ ⬅ ⬇. Then release the ⬆ key again.

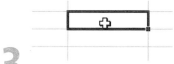

3 The cell can be deselected with a mouse-click anywhere on the worksheet.

Selecting individual cells

Mark 1		Mark 2	
	Mark 3		

1 Do you want to select individual cells which are **not next to each other**?

2 First press the ⌃Ctrl key and hold it down.

Mark 1		Mark 2	
	Mark 3		

3 Click on the individual cells one after the other.

Mark 1		Mark 2
	Mark 3	

4 Release the ⌃Ctrl key!

Deselect with a mouse-click anywhere on the worksheet.

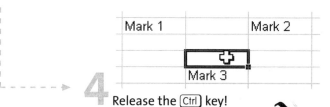

343

Selecting columns

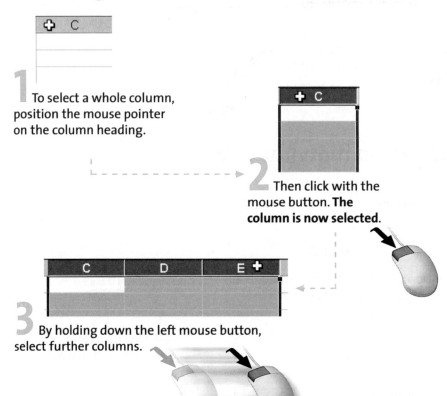

1 To select a whole column, position the mouse pointer on the column heading.

2 Then click with the mouse button. **The column is now selected.**

3 By holding down the left mouse button, select further columns.

Selecting rows

1 The procedure of selecting rows is the same as that for selecting columns. Position the mouse pointer on the row heading.

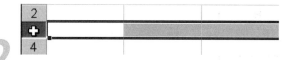

 Click once with the left mouse button. **The whole row is now selected.**

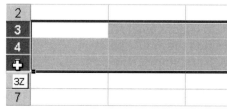

 By holding down the left mouse button you can select further rows.

Selecting the whole worksheet with a single click

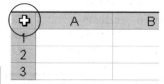

When you click on this place with the left mouse button, ...

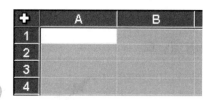 ... you select the whole worksheet.

345

	A	B
1		
2		
3		✛

3 Deselect with a click anywhere on the
worksheet.

Selecting cells for calculations

You can integrate individual cells in a calculation following the same
procedure as for 'normal' selection.

	A	B	C
1	Mon-Wed	Income	1000
2	Thur-Fri	Income	2000
3	Mon-Wed	Expenses	500
4	Thur-Sun	Expenses	450
5			
6	Mon-Sun	Income	
7			

1 Enter the data.

	A	B	C
1	Mon-Wed	Income	1000
2	Thur-Fri	Income	2000
3	Mon-Wed	Expenses	500
4	Thur-Sun	Expenses	450
5			
6	Mon-Sun	Income	✛
7			

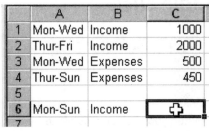

2 Activate the cell.

3 Click on the *AutoSum*
button.

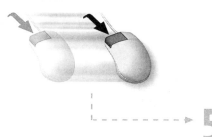

▼	×	✓	=	=SUM(C

	B	C
	Income	1000
	Income	2000

4 Select the cells you wish to calculate.

	A	B	C
1	Mon-Wed	Income	1000
2	Thur-Sun	Income	2000
3	Mon-Wed	Expenses	500
4	Thur-Sun	Expenses	450
5			
6	Mon-Sun	Income	3000
7			

5 Confirm with the ⏎ key.

But you can also calculate cells which are not next to each other.

	A	B	C	D
1	Turnover	5000	Costs	-4500
2				
3	Profit			

1 Type in the data.

	A	B	C	D
1	Turnover	5000	Costs	-4500
2				
3	Profit	⊕		

2 Click on the cell.

3 Activate the *AutoSum* button.

347

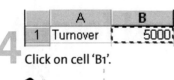

	A	B
1	Turnover	5000

4 Click on cell 'B1'.

5 Press the (Ctrl) key and keep holding it down.

	A	B	C	D
1	Turnover	5000	Costs	-4500
2				
3	Profit	=SUM(B1,D1)		

6 Click on cell 'D1'.

	A	B	C	D
1	Turnover	5000	Costs	-4500
2				
3	Profit	500		

7 Release the (Ctrl) key! Confirm with the (↵) key.

Numbers: entry and format

Numbers play a major role in a spreadsheet program such as Excel. That's what you calculate with after all!

A **format** is the appearance of a value as a currency or as a percentage.

However, especially the formats drive many beginners to despair.

With a few small exercises you will soon know everything about numbers and formats.

Where do you put the numbers?

1 Type a number into cell 'A1'.

	A
1	1111

2 Confirm the entry with the Formula bar.

3 A number value is always **right-aligned** in Excel. Instead, text is left-aligned. (See Chapter 2.)

	A
1	1111

You can format cells with *Align Left, Center,* and *Align Right* buttons.

Currencies

To apply a currency format, use the *Format Cells* dialog box or the *Currency* button.

> Before you can format a cell, you must select it by clicking on it first. If you want to format several cells, you need to select the corresponding cell range.

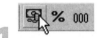

1 Click on the *Currency* button.

	A
1	£1,111.00

2 The value appears now as a currency (in this case: £).

> Format includes a 1000 separator and two decimal places

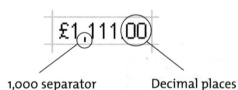

1,000 separator   Decimal places

On the *Format Cells* tab you can also specify other formats. Choose the FORMAT/CELLS menu option or press the Ctrl + 1 keyboard shortcut. Both take you to the same dialog box. (See Chapter 9.)

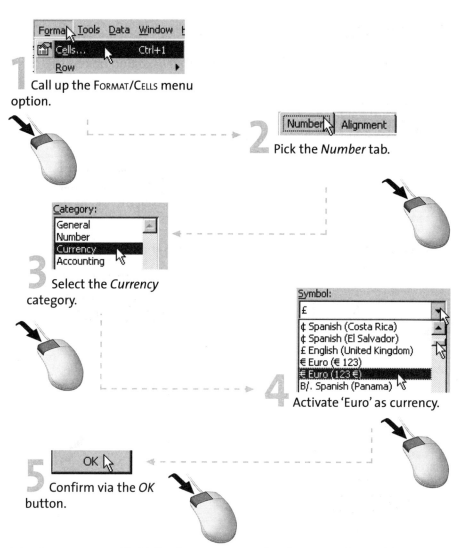

1 Call up the FORMAT/CELLS menu option.

2 Pick the *Number* tab.

3 Select the *Currency* category.

4 Activate 'Euro' as currency.

5 Confirm via the *OK* button.

Via the *Format Cells* dialog box you can also format cells with other **currencies**. For example, when you buy tulips from Amsterdam, you will format the cells 'hfl', so that the value appears as Dutch guilders.

You can also apply the following formats: number of units (for production, on an assembly line, eggs in your hen-house), measuring units (litres of beer or petrol consumption, metres in road construction).

How do you delete a format?

.... that is the question. First the wrong way, which especially Excel beginners often choose.

1 Press the Del key.

2 The value in cell 'A1' has disappeared.

When you now enter a new value into the cell the format specified last is automatically applied.

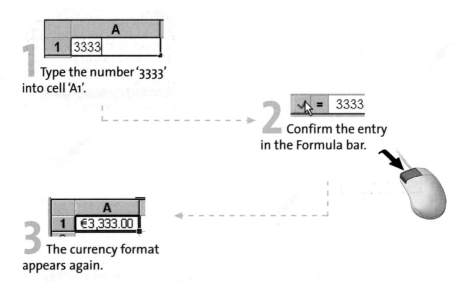

1 Type the number '3333' into cell 'A1'.

2 Confirm the entry in the Formula bar.

3 The currency format appears again.

When you want to delete a currency format, you do not delete it with the Del key, but you choose the *Format Cells* dialog box. Under *Category* you specify the required format, for example 'Standard'. In this way you are back to a 'normal' cell format.

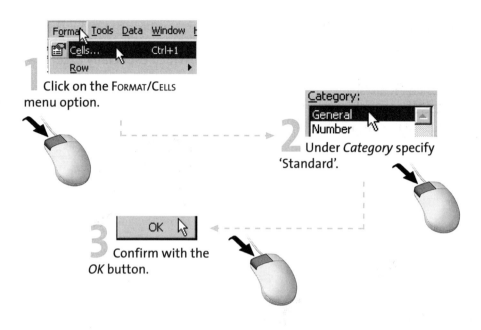

Click on the FORMAT/CELLS menu option.

Under *Category* specify 'Standard'.

Confirm with the *OK* button.

The 1,000 separator

The number '1000' can be displayed with or without a thousand separator '1,000'. You can enter the separator on the keyboard.

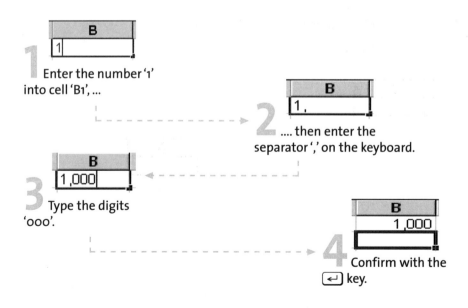

Enter the number '1' into cell 'B1', ...

.... then enter the separator ',' on the keyboard.

Type the digits 'ooo'.

Confirm with the ⏎ key.

An alternative way which leads to the same result is offered by the *Comma Style* button.

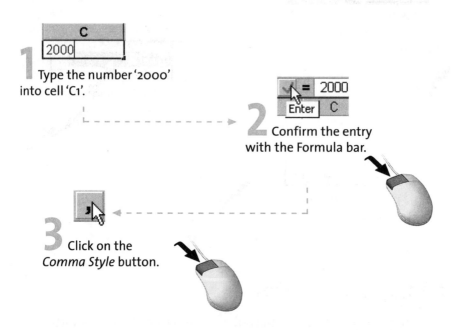

1 Type the number '2000' into cell 'C1'.

2 Confirm the entry with the Formula bar.

3 Click on the *Comma Style* button.

As a default, there are two zeros after the decimal point.

The numbers after the point: decimal places

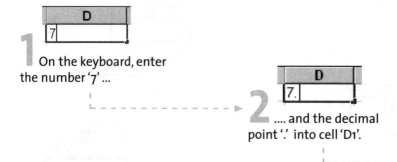

1 On the keyboard, enter the number '7' ...

2 .... and the decimal point '.' into cell 'D1'.

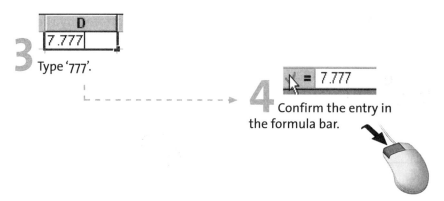

3 Type '777'.

4 Confirm the entry in the formula bar.

When you wish to add decimal places (1.23) one by one, you can click on the *Increase Decimal* button. For each mouse-click, one decimal place (1.234) is added.

Correspondingly, you can delete decimal places (1.234) with the *Decrease Decimal* (1.23) button.

Excel automatically rounds up/down accordingly. (See Chapter 12.)

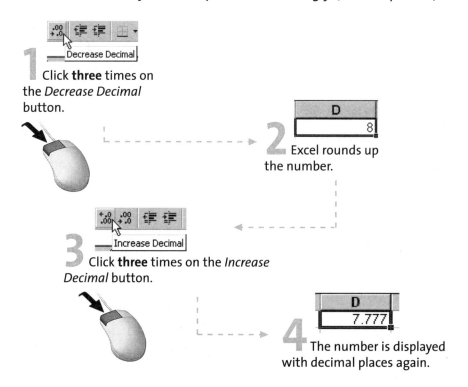

1 Click **three** times on the *Decrease Decimal* button.

2 Excel rounds up the number.

3 Click **three** times on the *Increase Decimal* button.

4 The number is displayed with decimal places again.

In per cent

In business, in elections, on food packaging, or when purchasing alcoholic drinks, percentage values are part of everyday life.

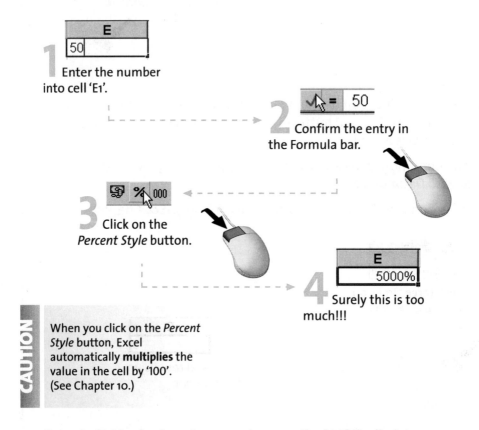

1 Enter the number into cell 'E1'.

2 Confirm the entry in the Formula bar.

3 Click on the *Percent Style* button.

4 Surely this is too much!!!

When you click on the *Percent Style* button, Excel automatically **multiplies** the value in the cell by '100'. (See Chapter 10.)

Enter individual values in percentage on the keyboard.

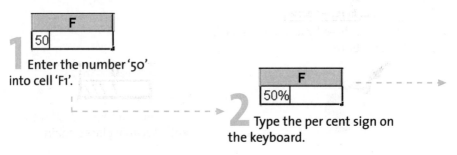

1 Enter the number '50' into cell 'F1'.

2 Type the per cent sign on the keyboard.

F
50%

 3 Confirm the entry
with the ⏎ key. The
value is displayed in per
cent style.

When you enter the number
'0.5' and click on the *Percent
Style* button, Excel will convert
it to '50 %'.

Answers

Chapter 2

Which command sequence activates ScreenTips?

- ❏ FORMAT/FONT/SCREENTIPS
- ❏ VIEW/TOOLBARS/CUSTOMIZE/ *SCREENTIPS* tab
- ☒ VIEW/TOOLBARS/CUSTOMIZE/ *OPTIONS/DISPLAY SCREENTIPS on toolbars tab*

How are cell names structured?

- ❏ FIRST THE **CELL** AND THEN THE **COLUMN** IS LISTED.
- ☒ FIRST THE **COLUMN** AND THEN THE **ROW** LISTED.
- ❏ FIRST THE **ROW** AND THEN THE **COLUMN** IS LISTED.

What does the mouse pointer look like when it is in an Excel worksheet?

- ☒   ⊕
- ❏   I
- ❏   ↖

Chapter 3

I. EXERCISE

Which sign do you need to enter in front of a calculation?

- ☒   =
- ❏   None.
- ❏   '

II. Exercise

Which signs are used for the various arithmetical operations in Excel?

- + * / \ x X

Division: /

Addition: +

Multiplication: *

Subtraction: -

III. Exercise

C2:C4 – The sign ':' means:

☒   C2 to C4

❑   C2 divided by cell C4

❑   C2 or C4

☒   The cell range C2 to C4

VI. Exercise

Account	500	←	=C3*0.1
10% Discount	50		
Total	450	←	=C3-C4

Chapter 5

	A	B	C	D	E
1	**Private Budget**				
2					
3	**Expenses**				
4	Flat(Rent)	1200		1200	
5	Electricity and Gas	350		350	
6	Mortgage	250		250	
7	Insurance	150		150	
8	Sports Club	80		80	
9	Food	400		400	
10	Dog Food	40		40	
11	Clothing	400		400	
12	Car	250		250	
13	Miscellaneous	200		200	
14	Sum of Expenses	3320		=SUM(B4:B13)	
15					
16	**Income**				
17	Net income	5000		5000	
18	Extra Income	400		400	
19	Sum of Income	5400		=SUM(B17:B18)	
20					
21	**Income Surplus**	2080		=SUM(B19-B14)	

Chapter 6

Clicking on the *Open* button and the FILE/OPEN menu option lead ...

❑ to different dialog boxes

❑ to the *Open* dialog box

☒ to the *Save* dialog box

For read- and write-protection the password is ...

❑ important

☒ unimportant

A workbook can only be deleted, ...

❑ when it is open, i.e. currently in use

☒ when it is not open, i.e. currently not in use

Calculating and comparing in Excel

Sign	Meaning
+	Addition
-	Subtraction
-	Negative value
*	Multiplication
/	Division
%	Conversion into per cent
^	Exponentiation
=	Equal
<	Less than
>	More than
<=	Less equal
>=	More equal
<>	Unequal

Error messages

Error messages always begin with the character '#'. Excel displays them in the cell containing the formula or instruction which could not be executed.

Message	Meaning	Solution
#########	The column is too narrow to display the expression/value.	Increase the column width.
#Div/o!	Mathematically incorrect: Numbers cannot be divided by 'o'.	Check the cell contents. All values must be different from 'o'.
#Name?	Excel does not recognise the formula text.	You have entered the wrong name (of cells/ cell ranges). Amend it in the Formula bar.
#Zero!	Individual cells or cell ranges do not agree with each other.	Check the characters in the formula or function (; :) or the cell entries. (A1, B2, C3 and so on.)
#NV	A value is not available in a function or formula.	Check the contents of the function, formula, or cells.
##VALUE!	The formula or function cannot be executed because of a wrong data entry.	You have probably entered text instead of numbers.
#NUM!	There is a problem with a number.	Check the number values in the formula or function, or in the cells.

Glossary

3D
Some chart types use three-dimensional elements to display the number values graphically. There are, among others, 3D bars, 3D columns, 3D areas, and even 3D surfaces. In Excel you can change chart types at any time. (Chapter 11)

Absolute field references
Field references are important when you copy formulas. An absolute field reference instructs Excel to refer to one and the same cell, as opposed to the relative field reference. (Chapter 9)

Access protection
This function restricts access to documents by users. Only users who know the write/read password are able to open documents.

You can set up or edit access protection by activating the *Options* button when saving a document with the FILE/SAVE AS menu command. (Chapter 6)

Advanced Filter
Under Excel you can use the filter to extract specific data by means of criteria. (Chapter 14)

Arguments
Specify what a function must work with. (Chapter 12)

Arrow
An arrow can be added to every chart. This element allows specific facts, such as a trend, to be more clearly identified. The arrow symbol with which you activate the function can be found on the Drawing toolbar. (Chapter 11)

Auditing
A toolbar with buttons for selecting cells, which refer to an active cell or are causing an error.

The commands and the toolbar can be shown with the TOOLS/AUDITING menu. (Chapter 15)

363

AutoFill

A program function that can be executed in two ways: enter the first value of the series (for example a date or a time) into a cell, select it together with several cells below or beside it, then select the *Series* option under Edit/Fill.

Using the fill handle at the right bottom corner of the cell highlight is a lot quicker. Simply drag downwards while pressing the mouse button. (Chapter 7)

AutoFilter

You can prevent the display of specific data records, by filtering them according to certain criteria. (Chapter 14)

Borders

With Format/Cells on the *Borders* tab a border consisting of one or several lines of various weights and colours can be inserted around the selected cells.

A border is a formatting which is not deleted with the cell contents. Choose Edit/Clear/All, to remove the borders. You can also insert or remove borders with the *Borders* button in the Formatting toolbar. (Chapter 13)

Buttons

1.) Usually a component of dialog boxes. For example, you could confirm the selected options in a dialog box by clicking on the *OK* button. By clicking on the *Cancel* button you exit the dialog box without changing anything. (Chapter 2)

2.) A button in the toolbars represents a function (for example the shape of a printer for printing).

Calculation

Calculate = 'compute, assess'. From the Latin word *calculare* (literal translation: to handle counting stones). (Chapter 2)

Category

That is what Excel calls the contents of the X axis of a chart, which in practice usually consists of the first row or column of the displayed cell range. (Chapter 11)

Cell protection

By activating the cell protection function you can prevent the accidental modification of cell contents. However, any user can intentionally change it, as this function is not password-protected. (Chapter 6)

Cell range

Several cells together form a cell range. (Chapter 3)

Cells

In Excel the boxes where columns and rows intersect are called 'cells'. (Chapter 2)

Chart Wizard

Helps you to select from various chart types (column , pie, and so on) and to create charts from your tables. (Chapter 11)

Circular references

When a formula directly or indirectly refers to the cell containing the formula, this is called circular reference. (Chapter 12)

Clipboard

The clipboard is usually used by Windows to move or copy text. With the COPY or CUT commands the text is stored on the clipboard and can be inserted when required (with the PASTE command).

Comment

A comment is a remark, which is inserted into a text. You can enter a comment for each cell in a table. Comments permit the insertion of additional information which does not appear in a table. As well as text comments, you can also record an audio comment in Excel. However, for recording comments, you need a sound card and a microphone.
Comments can be shown or hidden with the VIEW/COMMENTS command.

Colour

Nowadays colour plays an important part in spreadsheets. You can use coloured elements in cells, text, and charts. The way you define the colour depends on the element you wish to colour. There is also an option to colour negative values automatically. (Chapter 13)

Colour palette

The colour palette offers you a selection of various colours in the shape of small colour boxes. A single mouse-click on one of the boxes is sufficient to select a colour. (Chapter 13)

Column

A column stands for the vertical plane in a table. They are addressed by letters: A, B, C, ... (Chapter 2)

Condition

With a condition you formulate an expression. The prerequisite for the execution of instructions, which are assigned to this condition, is that the expression is TRUE. If the expression is FALSE, the instructions are skipped or alternative instructions are carried out. In Excel you define conditions with the function IF(). (Chapter 13)

Context menu

Right-clicking the mouse opens a Context menu. The name refers to the fact that the composition of the individual menu items is dependent on the context or the situation in which the mouse button is pressed. (Chapter 2)

Cursor

An on-screen position indicator in form of a flashing vertical line or an arrow. It indicates the place where the next input by the user will appear.

Cut

Cutting moves the selected text or the selected objects onto the clipboard, from where they can be pasted into other documents or document areas, but also into other program windows. The difference with the copying function is that the original is deleted when cutting. (Chapter 4, 7 and 9)

Database

A database is an organised collection of associated data, for example addresses. (Chapter 14)

Data field

A data field is the smallest independent unit of a database. One or more data fields make up a data record. An address record for example could be made up of the data fields name, first name, street, and town. (Chapter 14)

Data form

A data form is a dialog box in which the fields of a database can be easily edited. (Chapter 14)

Data map

A program with which you can create map objects to display Excel data geographically. Click on the *Map* button on the standard toolbar to create a map for the selected data range.

Data medium

A data medium is a storage medium, for example a diskette or a hard disk, on which you can permanently store your folder. (Chapter 5)

Data record

Consists of data fields ('name, first name, street, town' and so on) and is a part of a database such as 'addresses'. (Chapter 14)

Date

Excel uses an internal calendar. The program retrieves the current date from the system clock of the computer or from the settings of the Windows system control.

=NOW()   Time and date

=TODAY()   Date
(Chapter 9)

Dialog boxes

They are used for inputting data and for selecting commands. Thus, there is a dialogue between you – the user – and Excel. (Chapter 2)

Directory

Directories are like the drawers of a cupboard (=hard disk). All files which belong together are put into the same drawer (=directory). (Chapter 5)

Diskettes

These data media can record and permanently store computer data through a floppy disk drive, which is also used for reading them again when you need to retrieve the data. (Chapter 5)

Diskette write-protection

Diskettes have a write-protection option. If the small black switch is in the upper position (the 'small window' is open), files can be read from the diskette but it is not possible to write to it.

In this way, the data stored on the diskette cannot be accidentally deleted. If you push the switch down, the data can be overwritten. (Chapter 5)

Drag and drop

Graphical user interfaces, such as Windows, offer this procedure, which allows you to move the mouse pointer onto an icon, hold down the mouse button and then drag the icon to a different position. (Chapter 4)

Drop-down list

This only becomes visible when you click on the button with the downward pointing arrow. Then you choose one element from a displayed list. (Chapter 2)

Entering formulas

A formula begins with an equal sign. (Chapter 2)

Error message

A computer report that warns you that a certain action cannot be executed or that there is something wrong with the processes currently running on your computer. If you need to ask somebody for help, note down the text of the error message and the corresponding error code (if available). (Chapter 12)

Error values

A value which is inserted into cells by Excel, when the contained formula cannot provide a correct result because it contains a logical error or the references point to cells containing the wrong data type or to empty cells. In Excel, error values always begin with the character '#'. (Chapter 13)

File

It includes all data (digits, letters, and so on), which are stored under a filename on a data medium (hard disk or diskette). To create files with Word, use the *Save* button or the FILE/SAVE or FILE/SAVE AS commands. (Chapter 5)

F1

Function key, which activates the online help in most programs.

File name

A filename consists of the name and its comment. Excel automatically assigns the extension '.xls'. (Chapter 5)

Folder

Hard disks, diskettes and CD ROMs are often (usually) divided into folders, which in turn can contain subfolders.

Windows Explorer and the dialog box of the FILE/SAVE menu command show these in form of folder icons.

To save a file in a folder double-click on its icon before you enter the file name and confirm with *Save*. (Chapter 6)

Formatting toolbar

By means of this toolbar you can apply so-called 'formatting', that is, you can, for example, choose a different font, display numbers as per cent values, or highlight text with *Bold* or *Underline*.

Formatting

This determines the attributes (for example bold, italic, font) for the appearance of a text on the screen and the print-out. (Chapter 4)

Formula

In Excel, this is a calculation which is entered with an equal sign. (Chapter 2)

Formula bar

Here you can see the contents of the active cell and edit cell entries (text, numbers, and formulas). (Chapter 2)

Hard disk

The hard disk is (as a rule) a built-in memory device, which allows storage of large amounts of data, even if the computer is switched off. (Chapter 5)

Header and footer

Text which is located at the top (the header) or at the bottom (the footer) of the page.

Italic

A font which slightly *tilts to the right*. (Chapter 4)

Legend

A legend contains descriptions of the elements of a chart. (Chapter 11)

List

Closed area of a table. (Chapter 14)

Load

To open a document. (Chapter 6)

Macro

A sequence of recorded or written commands, which trigger operations and are processed in sequence when called up.

Memory size

The number of Bytes (= characters), which are available on a hard disk or a diskette for the storage of data or programs. (Chapter 15)

Menu bar

Here you execute commands such as 'save, print, exit' by left-clicking on them with the mouse. (Chapter 1)

Online help

Program functions which helps to solve problems. (Chapter 15)

Operator

An operator is a sign with which you determine how two expressions (such as Numbers) are supposed to be linked or compared. (Chapter 13)

Option

Changes the settings of Excel 2000. Options are usually activated with a tab. (Chapter 2)

Page Preview

Before you print out a file you should check the result in the Print Preview via (FILE/PRINT PREVIEW or the *Print Preview* button). The Print Preview displays a document exactly as it will look in print. Excel literally 'prints out' on screen and uses all available fonts and formatting options available to the connected printer. (Chapter 5)

Pagebreak

The place in a document where one page ends and the next starts.

Pagebreak Preview

A view in which all the pagebreaks are shown and may be moved. The tables are displayed as reduced on the printing pages, so that the position of the pagebreaks and the print sequence can be checked and modified.

Activate it with VIEW/PAGEBREAK PREVIEW or the button in Print Preview mode. (Chapter 5)

Password

Identification code for the use of software or services. (Chapter 6)

Print range

When you print out a table without specifying a print range, Excel will print all cells that contain data.

To print a specific range, select this range and choose FILE/PRINT AREA/SET PRINT AREA. If you wish to print out disconnected ranges, press the [Ctrl] key while selecting. (Chapter 5)

Print

Printing a table or the displayed chart is carried out on a printer installed in Windows. In Excel you need to specify in advance the pages, the number of copies, and so on that you wish to print in the FILE/PRINT dialog box. (Chapter 5)

Properties

Additional information which is stored with a document, for example, statistical information about processing time, size, print, memory, and dynamic data, and optional entries such as title, author, keywords, or comments. (Chapter 5)

Query

A query is carried out in a database. For example, you can extract all customers whose name starts with 'M' and/or live in a specific postal area. (Chapter 13)

Range address

The range address consists of the co-ordinates of a cell range. Thus, a range address, for example, may be: C3:C5. (Chapter 3)

Redo

Click on the button *Redo* to execute a command you have previously cancelled with the *Undo* button. (Chapter 2)

Reference

A reference is a cell address or a cell range in a table. There is a distinction between absolute and relative references.

Absolute means that the cell or the cell range itself is referred to, whereas a relative reference only records the path to the cell.

The absolute reference is used so that cell references do not change when copying. (Chapter 9)

Result

The result of a formula is always displayed in the cell that contains the formula. (Chapter 4)

Rotate

In Excel 2000 you can rotate the data of a cell 90 degrees to the right or left. Text rotation is possible with the FORMAT/CELLS command in the *Orientation* tab.

Row

Rows form the horizontal plane of a table. A row consists of neighbouring cells. Cells are addressed by numbers (1,2,3, ...). (Chapter 2)

ScreenTips

This feature provides information about what the numerous icons of Excel stand for. Whenever the mouse pointer rests for longer than a second on a button, a description of the button is displayed. (Chapter 2)

Scroll bar

The scroll bars at the right and bottom screen margin are used to scroll quickly through a document. (Chapter 2)

Sheet tabs

Located at the bottom screen margin, they display the names of the worksheet in a workbook. (Chapter 13)

Shortcuts

These are links to programs, folders, or files. When you call up the shortcut to Word, the program starts as if you had called it up with the Start menu. Shortcuts shorten processing time in Windows.(Chapter 1)

Standard toolbar

The buttons on the standard toolbar represent commands, which can also be executed with the menu. (Chapter 2)

Subtotals

An Excel function, with which you can analyse lists and table rows with identical entries grouped into categories. You can activate the function with the DATA/SUBTOTALS command. Before you activate it, you need to sort the table.

Sum

The standard function of the Excel table with its own separate button. Select the cell under or next to the area you want to add up, and click on the sigma sign.

Excel automatically marks the range of the cells you want to add up. Confirm it with a mouse-click.

The function runs as follows: =SUM(Range)

To add up more than one range, specify the ranges with the separator semicolon:

=SUM(Range1; Range2). (Chapter 2)

Syntax

The structure of a formula. (Chapter 12)

Tab

To make dialog boxes as clear as possible, many are displayed as a kind of 'card file index', which contains various tabs. (Chapter 2)

Tables

In a table text and numbers are arranged into rows and columns. The individual boxes created by the intersections are called cells. (Chapter 2)

Table templates

You can only open a table template with the FILE/NEW menu option.

Title bar

Always indicates the document you are currently editing, or to put it in another way, the title (name) with which you are currently working. (Chapter 5)

Top 10

Lists the ten first data records after filtering: the highest numbers, per cent values, and so on. (Chapter 14)

Undo

This button undoes the last executed command. With each further click, one more command is undone. (Chapter 2)

Write-protection recommendation

Every user can switch off a write-protection recommendation. When you open a document with a write-protection recommendation, you will be asked whether you want to edit it write-protected or not. (Chapter 6)

Wildcard

This represents characters. That is, they are a replacement for parts of a filename, and thus permit the listing of a group of files. The two most common wildcards are '?' for a single character and '*' for an entire filename or part of it. (Chapter 14)

Wizard

Wizards help with the execution of certain steps, and assist the user to solve similarly structured tasks. The steps are outlined one by one, just like in a manual. (Chapter 11)

Workbook

The sheets with which you work in Excel are called a 'workbook'. (Chapter 5)

Worksheet

A worksheet contains rows and columns. It is, in a way, the basic entity you work with in Excel. (Chapter 1)

Zoom

The zoom function of Word reduces or magnifies the current screen display of a document.

Index

Symbols

198, 362
% 193
* 312
.xls extension 94
? 312

A

absolute references 170
absolute values 170
Access 10
access 119
activate
   auditing 327
   formula 330
   option 28
   table 208
   the Menu bar 13
   toolbars 24
active folders 118
add
   decimal places 241
adding list 206

The Standard toolbar

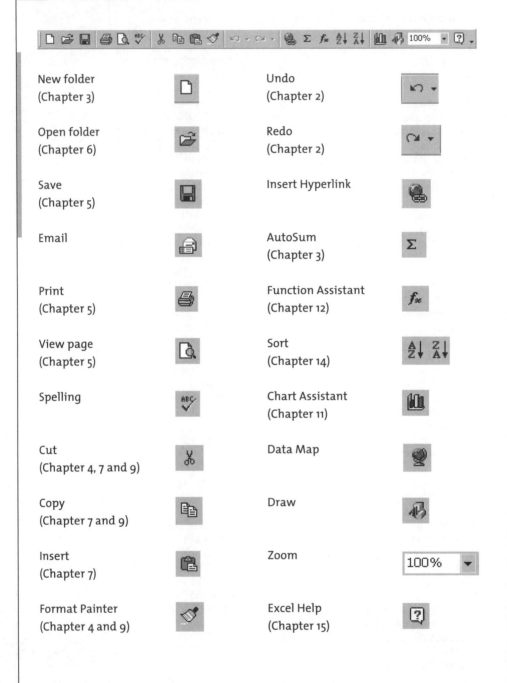

New folder (Chapter 3)		Undo (Chapter 2)	
Open folder (Chapter 6)		Redo (Chapter 2)	
Save (Chapter 5)		Insert Hyperlink	
Email		AutoSum (Chapter 3)	
Print (Chapter 5)		Function Assistant (Chapter 12)	
View page (Chapter 5)		Sort (Chapter 14)	
Spelling		Chart Assistant (Chapter 11)	
Cut (Chapter 4, 7 and 9)		Data Map	
Copy (Chapter 7 and 9)		Draw	
Insert (Chapter 7)		Zoom	100%
Format Painter (Chapter 4 and 9)		Excel Help (Chapter 15)	

The Format toolbar

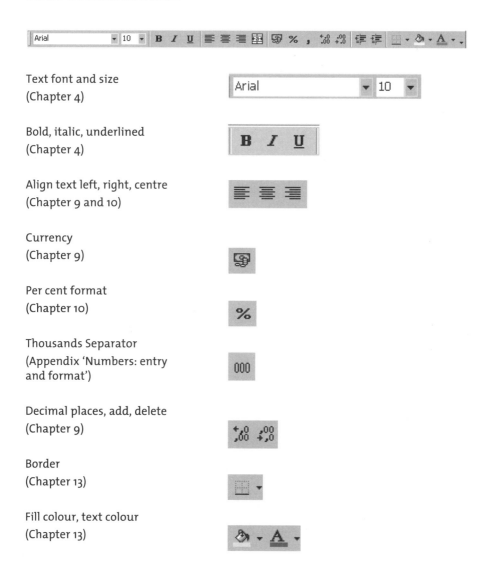

Text font and size
(Chapter 4)

Bold, italic, underlined
(Chapter 4)

Align text left, right, centre
(Chapter 9 and 10)

Currency
(Chapter 9)

Per cent format
(Chapter 10)

Thousands Separator
(Appendix 'Numbers: entry
and format')

Decimal places, add, delete
(Chapter 9)

Border
(Chapter 13)

Fill colour, text colour
(Chapter 13)